THE NORTON SERIES ON
SOCIAL EMOTIONAL LEARNING SOLUTIONS
PATRICIA A. JENNINGS, SERIES EDITOR

D1636957

NORTON BOOKS IN EDUCATION

Mindfulness in the Secondary Classroom

A Guide for Teaching Adolescents

PATRICIA C. BRODERICK

W. W. Norton & Company

Independent Publishers Since 1923

New York | London

For information about permission to reproduce selections from this book, write to Permissions, W. W. Norton & Company, Inc., 500 Fifth Avenue, New York, NY 10110

For information about special discounts for bulk purchases, please contact W. W. Norton Special Sales at specialsales@wwnorton.com or 800-233-4830

Manufacturing by Versa Press
Book design by Molly Heron
Production manager: Katelyn MacKenzie

Library of Congress Cataloging-in-Publication Data

Names: Broderick, Patricia C., author.
Title: Mindfulness in the secondary classroom :
a guide for teaching adolescents / Patricia C. Broderick.
Description: First edition. | New York : W.W. Norton & Company, [2019] |
Series: Norton books in education | Series: Social emotional learning solutions series |
Includes bibliographical references and index.
Identifiers: LCCN 2018052102 | ISBN 9780393713138 (pbk.)
Subjects: LCSH: Affective education. | Mindfulness (Psychology) | Emotional intelligence—
Study and teaching (Secondary) | Emotions and cognition. | Stress in adolescence. |
High school students—Psychology.
Classification: LCC LB1072 .B76 2019 | DDC 370.15/34—dc23 LC record available at
https://lccn.loc.gov/2018052102

W. W. Norton & Company, Inc., 500 Fifth Avenue, New York, N.Y. 10110
www.wwnorton.com

W. W. Norton & Company Ltd., 15 Carlisle Street, London W1D 3BS

1 2 3 4 5 6 7 8 9 0

For Connor, Owen,
Wesley, and Will—
and for all our children

Contents

From the Series Editor

I am thrilled to introduce the first volume in this new book series from Norton Books in Education: SOCIAL AND EMOTIONAL LEARNING SOLUTIONS. The SEL Solutions Series features compact books for educators focused on recommended SEL practices from experts in the field. Cutting-edge research continues to confirm that instruction in social and emotional skills pays off in improved behavior and academic learning while students are in school, and that these skills continue to contribute to their success as adults. The books are intended to provide school leaders and classroom teachers with SEL tools and strategies that are grounded in research yet highly accessible, so readers can confidently begin using them to transform school culture, improve student behavior, and foster learning with the proven benefits of SEL.

As a former teacher and school leader, I am familiar with the challenge of finding the time to parse the theory and sift through research to identify the practices that will be effective in the classroom. The intention with this set of books is to circumvent this problem by tapping into the work of those who have already done the parsing and sifting: to have experts in the field of SEL present trustworthy concepts succinctly and emphasize applications and activities that can be implemented right away, without needing to adopt a separate program or curriculum. Our aim is to provide a set of quick, appealing, read-in-one-sitting guides to address different aspects of SEL implementation in classrooms, schools, and districts.

Patricia Broderick's book *Mindfulness in the Secondary Classroom: A Guide for Teaching Adolescents* is a magnificent overture to this new series. Drawing on her years of experience as a secondary teacher, mindfulness instructor, SEL program developer, and researcher, Broderick has woven a tapestry of important concepts and practical strategies to help educators promote whole-adolescent development. Recognizing that in SEL the teacher is the curriculum, she emphasizes the importance of adults as role models for the mindfulness, compassion, and social and emotional competencies we want our students to learn. Broderick highlights the importance of SEL development in adolescence, when our students are exploring identity, values, and life's meaning, and she provides developmentally appropriate ways to introduce mindful awareness and compassion practices to support this developmental stage. As she notes, the risky behavior common to adolescents is usually rooted in an attempt to avoid unpleasant emotions; practicing mindfulness promotes the ability to accept such feelings, without judgement, and increases students' ability to tolerate and work with their full range of emotions. Indeed, Broderick's years of research have proven that teaching developmentally appropriate mindful awareness and compassion practices to adolescents helps them learn to manage stress, improve emotion regulation, and promote their own well-being.

Patricia A. Jennings
Editor, Norton Series on Social and Emotional Learning Solutions

Acknowledgments

I wish to express my sincere gratitude to the teachers and other educational professionals I have been fortunate to meet through my work in the field of mindfulness in education. As a former secondary school teacher myself, I have deep admiration for the work they do and am inspired by the dedication this work requires. In their day-to-day interactions with students and families, these educators translate the values of service and love into something very present and very real. I hope this book offers them support and a set of practices that deepen their commitment and empower them in their lives. May the benefits of their own mindfulness practice accrue to the youth in their care and revitalize the institutions in which they work.

I also wish to thank Carol Collins, my editor at Norton, for her expertise and support as this book was being written. Her thoughtful suggestions have made this book a better one. Gratitude also goes to Tish Jennings,

Series Editor, and to all the Norton staff: Kevin Olsen, Megan Bedell, Nicholas Fuenzalida, as well as Mariah Eppes and Sara McBride, whose careful attention to these chapters both clarified and improved the manuscript.

Finally, my deepest appreciation goes to my husband, my children, and grandchildren for their steadfast love, energy, and presence, and for the joy they bring to me in each moment.

Mindfulness in the Secondary Classroom

Mindfulness: Educational Fad or Effective Practice?

Mindfulness is having a moment. From its place on the cover of *Time* magazine to its advocacy by celebrities, we've heard its praises sung by people from many different walks of life. But what is it, anyway? And, does it deserve all the hype? What, if anything, does mindfulness have to offer to teachers in secondary schools? If you reflect on some of the ways the term mindfulness has been used, you might conclude that it's a gimmick or a quick fix. It's been used to describe products from cosmetics, to mayonnaise, to coloring books. Many previously innocuous activities, like working out or financial investing, are now publicized as "mindful." Advertisers appear to be convinced that mindfulness sells, hence the remarkable ubiquity of the term.

Educators may be particularly sensitive to the pernicious effect of quick fixes. Even teachers who are relatively new to the field of education have witnessed the comings and goings of pedagogical trends that can be as frustrating to implement as they are short-lived. Is mindfulness just another fad that will run its course in due time?

We don't know the answer yet, but it's important to note that mindfulness has been around for a very long time. In fact, the term comes from ancient Eastern cultural traditions and derives from the verb: *to remember*, or to *take mental note*. Although classical Eastern texts have contributed a precise and detailed explication of mindfulness, its practice, and its role in helping people with the stress of life, mindfulness is not owned by any one cultural tradition. Just as algebra had its origins in Mesopotamia, a region that corresponds to modern-day Iraq and Syria, we recognize that mindfulness is a human advance developed by an ancient culture that has benefited us all. One of the great pioneers of present-day mindfulness teaching is Jon Kabat-Zinn, a research scientist who developed an 8-week mindfulness program originally for chronic pain patients at the University of Massachusetts Medical Center. He wisely distilled the essence of mindfulness into an accessible format to help contemporary people with contemporary problems, such as physical pain and mental stress.

Research on mindfulness practice is becoming increasingly refined, and the burgeoning scholarship in this area highlights the problems associated with simplistic definitions of the term (Lutz, Jha, Dunne, & Saran, 2015). Although it's clear there are multiple dimensions to mindfulness, Kabat-Zinn's (1991) definition is one that is frequently used and easily accessible to most people. Simply put, mindfulness means *paying attention* to our experience *in a particular way.* It's surprising that how we pay attention is so important and can have such dramatic effects on health and well-being. When we speak with students, we use attention. When we make decisions, we use attention. When we grade tests or plan our lessons, we use attention. When we attend a lecture, play sports, argue a point, or prepare a meal, we use attention. Perhaps there is no more common teacher directive than "pay attention!" Attention is the common denominator of all kinds of learning, and learning is fundamentally an internal process, despite the best techniques and technologies that teachers can find to inform and motivate students. What we may be less likely to attend to is the *quality* of our attention, for attention has a range of characteristic descriptors such as flexible, clear, dull, or scattered.

Mindfulness is paying attention intentionally (on purpose) to what is actually happening right now (present moment), both inside and outside us in a way that is accepting, compassionate, open, and curious (nonjudgmental) (see Kabat-Zinn, 1991). These qualities of mindfulness, intentional, present-focused, and nonjudgmental illustrate that mindful attention is different from a laserlike hyperfocus that suppresses awareness of everything else that's happening; from being what is called "spaced out" and only partly conscious, or from being caught up in our own mental worlds. It is here and now *attention with attitude*: curious, open, and accepting. Mindfulness includes qualities of mind *and* heart, thus securing its place as a strong foundation for other social and emotional skills.

MY MINDLESS LIFE

The alarm didn't go off, so Jim wakes up later than usual. He's relieved that it's only 20 minutes past his usual time, given how exhausted he feels. He scrambles to get dressed, into the car, and off to work before the start of his first-period class. No time to stop for his regular coffee, he thinks. As he pulls out of his driveway, thoughts of last evening's interaction with his teenage son fill his mind. *What was that kid thinking taking the family car and staying out so late, getting an expensive parking ticket in the process*? He knows that his son has a major test today and is not hopeful about his prospect of passing. Jim fumes about his son's irresponsibility and remembers all the occasions he's had to deal with his son's adolescent shenanigans. Jim's thoughts move to some of his less responsible students, who remind him of his son. His mind trails off as he replays the events. Suddenly, he notices that he is driving past the school entrance. How did he get to school already? He can't remember a thing about his drive.

You may be wondering if mindful attention is something that is possible for you. In fact, we all have the capacity to be mindful. Take a moment to remember a time when your attention was truly and wholeheartedly present with an experience as it was occurring. You were fully engaged, receptive, and open to the totality of the experience, body and mind. Perhaps it was a special moment with a child, a student, or a loved one, maybe noticing a beautiful natural setting, or even something painful, when you were open to the whole of the circumstance. You were experiencing it in the moment, as it occurred, with awareness of its sensory and emotional dimensions.

It might be surprising to learn that mindfulness is described as a way of paying attention, because many people associate mindfulness with relaxation. People often assume that if someone is pleasantly relaxed, then that person is being mindful. When a person is not feeling pleasantly relaxed, perhaps because of pain, exhaustion, frustration, or something similar, then he or she is not being mindful. Conflating feeling pleasantly relaxed, as you might feel during a massage or a walk in the woods, with mindfulness is a misunderstanding. Certainly, we hope that practicing mindfulness can help us become more relaxed and less stressed, as has been borne out by years of research. However, it is crucial to understand that practicing mindfulness *in order to* have any particular experience, like relaxation, is not the goal. Mindfulness is a much more expansive construct than simply a transient pleasant feeling. This is why Kabat-Zinn and others refer to mindfulness as a *way of being,* a practice of opening mind and heart for greater awareness and attunement to oneself, other people, and aspects of the world.

There are a few reasons to take this information to heart. First, you and your students might abandon any attempt to practice mindfulness if the initial efforts do not result in feeling relaxed right away. You might determine that mindfulness is not for you, and this can be a potentially unhelpful conclusion. Second, we often judge ourselves quite harshly if we can't achieve a state of relaxation or peacefulness. Our self-criticism can become an obstacle to the kind of nonjudgmental awareness that mindfulness is intended to cultivate. Third, rigid expectations for achieving some predetermined outcome, like relaxation, can interfere with the authentic openness to experience that truly leads to greater stress reduction and emotional balance.

All this being said, most people do become curious about mindfulness because they recognize the stress burden they carry, and they want to feel better. So, it's not unusual or inappropriate to practice mindfulness in order to cultivate greater well-being and more positive, wholesome qualities in our lives. Teaching is among the most stressful of all the professions, filled with daily uplifts and struggles. It involves a profound opportunity to have a positive impact on young people as they mature into adulthood. It offers the potential for connection, discovery, and pride in student accomplishments on a daily basis. But it can also be also a round of daily frustrations that occur within busy institutions that neither allow teachers much control nor provide enough support. Teaching is demanding and relentlessly time-consuming, with endless paperwork and daily concerns about students' well-being. At times, teachers are viewed as the cause of all the problems in the educational system, so their self-efficacy may be shaken. And all of these circumstances might be part of a day's work. A recent study by the American Federation of Teachers (2017) reported a massive increase in the amount of stress that teachers report. New teachers leave the profession in alarmingly high numbers. Some say there is a teaching crisis in education (Carver-Thomas & Darling-Hammond, 2017). Can mindfulness practice really make any difference, given all of this?

As effective as many educational techniques and strategies can be, they don't necessarily resolve all the challenges of teaching and don't impact all of the students, all of the time. Teachers can purchase educational materials, arrange classrooms, set up group activities, compose objectives, and create assessments. They can read all the latest research in their fields and understand theories of teaching and learning. They can be knowledgeable about adolescent development. Yet, they may still find themselves struggling with students who are unmotivated or rebellious. Teachers might worry about their own commitment or doubt their ability to reach young people or to satisfy superiors. They might start to feel burned out from the daily grind of classroom demands.

As you know, this book is part of a Social and Emotional Learning Solutions series for teachers and school leaders. The concept behind this series raises an obvious question: To which problems of classroom teachers do social and emotional solutions apply? In contrast to relatively solvable problems like organizing classroom routines, dealing with the emotional needs that your students present every day is a more complex task—perhaps particularly complex for teachers of middle and high school students. Adolescent brain development is "under construction" and will continue steadily until the mid-to-late twenties. Areas of the brain related to self-control are less well developed than those involved in emotional reactivity, while risk taking in the service of autonomy also increases. This state of affairs contributes to the high degree of emotional volatility among adolescents as a group compared to people at other stages of the life span (Blakemore & Mills, 2014; Spear, 2013). So, your students are probably a little interpersonally challenging just by virtue of their being adolescents.

Skills in managing social and emotional issues, both your own and those of your students, are a necessary part of the secondary teacher's repertoire. Their absence can interfere with successful relationships and compassionate discipline and can add to the stress burden of teachers who work in a highly charged setting. Lack of these skills can impact the way you view your teaching effectiveness and affect your moods, health, and performance. Clearly, teaching involves more than being a well-organized and knowledgeable "talking head." Solutions for these difficult social and emotional problems require, by definition, well-developed social and emotional competence. Teaching is about relationships just as is it about academic content. It matters how your classroom is set up, how routines are established, and what technological tools are used. But it also matters that you are engaged, present, and responsive, because *you* are your most important teaching instrument. In addition to the skills and subject-area knowledge you possess, the quality of your mental and emotional well-being, your resilience, stress tolerance, your courage, and your purpose are profoundly important in this work. These social and emotional skills of emotional balance are the foundation for the caring classrooms we hope to create (Jennings & Greenberg, 2009).

LEARNING MY LIMITS

Sarah takes pride in the fact that she works hard, maybe harder than other teachers. She always tells herself that if she feels relaxed, with nothing to do, she isn't working hard enough. She is the person her principal can always call on for help. In addition to being the school liaison to community and parent groups and the faculty mentor for an after-school club, she pitches in when the principal or teachers need help with some project. Her latest extra task involves decorating the bulletin boards near the main office in preparation for the homecoming game. Because a friend encouraged her to take a mindfulness class, Sarah has recently begun practicing mindfulness. She's becoming more aware of the tension and stress in her body. It's gradually dawning on her that her body might be talking back to her and that she should listen. Perhaps she's been operating on automatic pilot? Her habit of overworking might be affecting her health. Sarah decides to take better care of herself. In a small but important first step, she tells her principal that she doesn't have time to decorate the bulletin boards this year.

Teaching adolescents requires a mode of mind that is open, curious, and accepting of the unexpected. The driver of this kind of teaching, then, may be your intentional presence, your willingness to "be here" moment after moment despite the challenging circumstances, and your inner poise in the midst of adolescent energy. This is where mindfulness practice can help.

Teachers and students alike all need to practice this way of paying attention to counteract the tendency to numb ourselves and just go through the motions. If mindfulness is about waking up to the moments of our lives, then perhaps most of the time we're a bit asleep. Another term for this is automatic pilot. As you will see in Chapter 3, being on automatic pilot has some harmful consequences. To become more mindful, present, and authentic, we first have to notice our tendency to be on automatic pilot. We have to notice when we're not paying attention, in its many manifestations. We have to wake up.

Because the mental habits of being lost in thought or on autopilot are so strong, we will intentionally practice the opposite skill set, the tools of mindful attention. With each additional chapter, this book will present more detail on what this means for you, for your teaching, and for your students. It will also offer some simple practices that you can use to develop mindfulness.

What You'll Find in the Rest of This Book

This book is structured to present, chapter by chapter, important aspects related to mindfulness and discuss their relevance to secondary school classrooms. Since mindfulness is for students and teachers alike, many of the examples used throughout refer to both youth and adults. Chapter 2 summarizes how our stress system operates and how we react to stressors in our lives. It makes a case for why we would want to practice mindfulness ourselves and teach it to adolescents. Chapters 3 through 7 describe features of mindful attention and offer ways to introduce, utilize, and practice these competencies. Each chapter includes two vignettes that illustrate how the main themes of the chapter apply to actual teachers and classrooms. The final sections of each chapter contain reflection questions, one or two formal practices related to chapter content, and a set of main points to take away.

Chapters 2 through 6 also include boxes entitled "Moving from Theory to Practice" that present practical tips about choosing programs, teacher training, ethical obligations, and whole-school implementation. These sections offer key points that teachers might wish to consider as they evaluate the possibility of introducing mindfulness to their students and their schools in a systematic manner. Finally, a way to increase the positive emotion of gratitude is offered as the concluding practice at the end of the book.

Reflecting on This Chapter

Try journaling your responses to the following questions:

What was my original understanding of mindfulness before I read this chapter?

How has my understanding changed (if at all) by reading this chapter?

How might the quality of my own attention affect my students and their performance?

In which circumstances am I most mindful? Most mindless?

**Questions available for download and printing at
http://wwnorton.com/rd/broderick**

Begin to Practice

A first step to becoming more mindful is to become aware of the moments in our lives when we are *mindless* or on automatic pilot. Let's start by exploring mindlessness in our lives. Remember to try, as best you can, to notice any automatic self-judging thoughts that might arise as you do this exercise.

Take some time, perhaps at the end of the day or before you go to bed, to reflect on what happened over the course of your day. Make an itemized list of your activities during that day. Then, on a scale of 0% (not at all mindful) to 100% (completely present), assess the level of mindful attention you paid to these activities. How much time during that day were you really present and aware? In which circumstances? During which activities were you least mindful?

Sample:

Activity	% Quality of Attention 0% ---------------------------------- 100% Mindless Mindful
Getting dressed	
Eating breakfast	
Driving to work	
Walking down the hall	
Proctoring an exam	
Other	

Tips to Take Away

Mindfulness is a way of paying attention, and mindlessness is inattention or automatic pilot. Mindfulness means paying attention, on purpose, in the present moment. Although mindfulness does foster relaxation, that is not its primary purpose. Mindfulness is a way of approaching all experience so that we are more present and more awake in our lives. To begin, you can take a moment to notice, as often as possible, how present you are. You might also introduce students to the idea that their attention has certain qualities: broad, narrow, focused, distracted, diffuse, stable, and so on. The quality of your attention and your willingness to be present to your students are critically important assets in your teaching.

The Problem of Stress and How Mindfulness Can Help

We know that mindfulness practice has benefitted many people based on their personal stories, but what justification might there be for its use with students and teachers in schools? We can look to the research community for some evidence. Psychologists as well as educators have shown great interest in this subject, and there has been a dramatic uptick in the number of articles about mindfulness published in scientific journals over time, from 1 article in 1982 to 692 in 2017 (American Mindfulness Research Association, 2018). Most research has been done with adults, but recent studies have also documented benefits for students. Although research in this field is still in its early stages, well-done meta-analyses (analyses of multiple studies) show improvements in secondary students' emotional wellness and cognitive processes. Overall, stress and anxiety are reduced, attentional processes are strengthened, and well-being is enhanced (Carsley, Khoury, & Heath, 2108; Felver, Celis-de Hoyos, Tezanos, & Singh, 2016; Klingbeil et al., 2017; Zoogman, Goldberg, Hoyt, & Miller, 2014). These gains are most apparent for students at risk; they show larger improvements because they are more likely to be in greater need. But even normally developing adolescents need our investment in their health and well-being (Dahl, Allen, Wilbrecht, & Suleiman, 2018). Thus, many prevention specialists believe the gains will come from the seeds teachers sow that bear fruit over time.

The purpose of this chapter is not to present an exhaustive overview of the research on mindfulness but rather to summarize why this topic has captured so much attention and explain how the findings can help you and your students. As we discussed in Chapter 1, stress reduction is one of the most basic reasons people are drawn to mindfulness, so we'll begin with an introduction to the relationship between mindfulness and stress.

Stress and the Brain

The modern science of *psychoneuroimmunology* originated during the last quarter of the 20th century. It explores the interaction between mind and body by examining the ways each communicates with the other in an intricate dance. The mind, nervous (brain and autonomic nervous system) and immune systems were first implicated in this communication network, although later work added the endocrine (hormonal) system. The new field of psycho-neuro-endocrine-immunology (Franca & Lotti, 2017) translates its understanding of the chemical language these systems use into applica-

MOVING FROM THEORY TO PRACTICE
The Importance of Training and
Personal Practice for Teachers

There is an ongoing and lively debate about who should teach mindfulness in schools. One thing to remember is that there is a difference between mindfulness practices (like mindful breathing or body scan) and mindfulness programs. Programs are sequenced, involve several sessions, and incorporate psychoeducation as well as mindfulness practices. An influential study found that the benefits of social and emotional learning (SEL) interventions on student outcomes were only found for students who participated in sequenced, research-based, and well-taught programs (Durlak, Dymnicki, Taylor, Weissberg, & Schellinger, 2011). This analysis also found that SEL programs taught by teachers, compared to outside experts, were most effective, presumably because of teachers' existing relationships with students and the teachers' opportunity to reinforce SEL skills on a daily basis. While some research suggests this is also the case for mindfulness programs, the evidence is mixed at this point (Carsley et al., 2018).

Although it remains an understudied question from a research perspective, it makes sense that teachers need personal experience with mindfulness, which is discussed in subsequent chapters, and training in the programs they teach. Some suggest that professional development for pre-service and practicing teachers should also include information about neuroscience (Ergas, Hadar, Albelda, & Levit-Binnun, 2018). Key tenets of this field are more than interesting tidbits of information. Rather, they illuminate the very processes of learning, the mechanisms of stress-related impediments to teaching and learning, and brain-based operations that influence well-being. Some critical points (e.g., that the brain is malleable, how stress affects learning, and why adolescence is a window of opportunity for brain development) can open secondary teachers' minds to the usefulness of mindfulness. For some people, the scientific doorway may be more accessible than one that initially immerses them in extended periods of contemplative practice. It provides a conceptual footing from which to recognize the value of personal practice and then to engage with it on a personal level. Ultimately, knowledge about mindfulness should support *but not replace* personal experience in mindfulness practice.

The more teachers know, the better able they will be to educate others about mindfulness. Teachers are on the frontline and may need to explain this practice to parents and other constituencies. As is the case with all educational programs, parents have the right to see curricular materials and know what's being taught to their children. A written curriculum, connected to educational objectives and available to parents, is a good way to make mindfulness practices transparent. Overall, educators should be good consumers of evidence, practiced and trained in mindfulness, and knowledgeable about any programs being delivered.

tions for prevention and treatment of disease. Notice that the mind plays a major role in this new field of integrative medicine, thus making this body of work relevant to the problem of stress and the importance of mindfulness.

If you were asked to identify what your stressors are, what would you say? If you're like most teachers, you'd probably mention lack of time; not enough money; too much responsibility at work; dealing with difficult students, colleagues, and parents; family concerns; and so on. If you asked your students, they might provide similar answers: problems with friends, families, or teachers; academic pressures; and safety concerns. Notice that all these responses involve external factors. So for most of us, our automatic assumption about stress is that it comes from factors outside ourselves.

There is no doubt that adverse external circumstances can provoke stress. Workplace conflicts, unruly students, demands for more and more standardized assessments, illness in the family, or challenges with one's own child are all external circumstances that can keep us up at night. It's the same for your students. It's difficult to be bullied or left out of a social group, to have more to do than you can manage, to live in poverty or in an unstable family situation that provides little support. Sometimes, a stressful event can threaten our very survival. It's alarmingly clear that we're living in an age of school shootings and other violent incidents. The most recent U.S. Department of Education survey indicates that approximately 95% of public schools now hold regular lockdown drills as safety precautions against armed intruders (Diliberti, Jackson, & Kemp, 2017). Many students and teachers no longer regard their school buildings as safe spaces. So, nothing in this book about mindfulness practice should be interpreted to suggest that there are no serious external threats to student and teacher safety or that we should tolerate harmful circumstances. We all need to act, as educators have always done, to support, protect, and nurture the youth in our care in reasonable ways and with concerted effort. Neither should mindfulness be viewed as a substitute for advocating more favorable working conditions or other school-based changes that address many of the reasons why students are suffering and why teachers are burning out and leaving the field in such high numbers (Podolsky, Kini, Bishop, & Darling-Hammond, 2016).

There is nothing wrong or abnormal about feeling stressed, even in less dangerous, more run-of-the-mill circumstances. Activating our body's stress response system is an absolutely vital function, because it informs us about potential danger and helps us cope. Our body-mind system produces the well-known fight-flight-freeze response that is supported by alterations in other physiological networks, like those regulating cardiovascular, immune, and metabolic functions (Sapolsky, 2004). The stress response system is essential when well used, but it can become dysregulated.

When stress is time-limited, the brain, autonomic, and other interrelated systems operate as they were designed to do, mobilizing resources to deal with a stressor and subsequently restoring balance. This flexibility, called *allostasis* (Sterling & Eyer, 1988), provides the capacity to cope effectively with many daily ups and downs. When stress is chronic, the system gets overworked and can shift toward a semipermanent state of activation (sensitization) or to one that mounts an insufficient (blunted) response. High levels of early life stress can play a role in sensitizing the stress system, orienting it to prefer one of these disordered response pathways over the other (Conradt, 2017; Danese & Baldwin, 2017). Teachers increasingly hear the terms "trauma" and "traumatized," which are often used to describe this phenomenon for certain students. Sadly, the effects of trauma and other adverse childhood experiences do not necessarily go away when children get to middle and high school. Research now shows that early life stress can be biologically embedded within our genetic makeup, opening the door to an array of adverse outcomes (Meaney, 2010).

SHARING STRESS: TEACHERS AND STUDENTS

Teachers have many sources of stress because of the demanding nature of the job. Mental perceptions, distorted through a self-critical or judgmental inner lens, are internal sources of stress. One teacher's version of a distorted inner lens might sound like this:

Everybody knows that stress is par for the course for a teacher. To complain about stress, when everyone else is feeling the same— it's just not right. It would be taking the easy way out. I'd be letting my colleagues down, because they're the ones who have to pick up the slack if I don't carry my weight. If my students don't achieve, it's my responsibility because they will be a problem for their next teacher. It means I've failed at my job. School systems don't make it easy for us teachers, though. My principal's classroom observations are supposed to help me improve, but they are nerve-racking. I can tell he doesn't have one good thing to say about what I'm doing. I can't help thinking that he takes his own stress out on me.

Students also have internal and external stressors that are unknown to teachers but that play out in the classroom. Consider what's happening in the life of this high school student:

Dan was always a good student who got mostly A's and B's when he was younger. In middle school, his grades started to slip. Now in high school he likes to play video games when he can. From his point of view, homework is a lot more boring than video games, so he puts it off until the last minute. Often he rushes out of the house without breakfast to catch the bus after oversleeping. Sometimes, he tries to do his homework on the bus, but his friends tease him and he just puts it away. Dan's stepfather has tried to crack down on Dan's poor school performance. He made Dan get a "real" job to teach him responsibility, instead of wasting hours on the computer. Dan works about 18 hours a week in a restaurant near his home. The other kids who work there are older, and they encourage him to party with them after work, which usually includes drinking. Dan's stepfather thinks he should have a career plan in place, but Dan has no idea what he wants to do when he graduates. Some of the kids at his school seem to have a much better idea about their future, a fact that makes Dan feel even more upset than he usually does. He tries not to think about it.

Teachers themselves are not immune from the early experience of inadequate care or adversity, so sometimes teachers' own physiological systems are also very reactive to stress. The level of societal stress and the high incidence of trauma in people's lives makes it a good bet that some of your students will have very high stress reactivity, often because of exposure to multiple and sustained adverse environmental impacts. *Allostatic load* (McEwen, 2013) is the term used to describe the wear and tear on our bodies and minds caused by prolonged activation of our stress systems. Some allostatic outcomes are manifested physiologically, as in chronically high blood pressure, heart rate, sleep disturbances, and metabolic syndrome. Some outcomes of chronic stress affect cognitive functions, such as attention problems, impaired memory, problems in learning, and compromised decision making. Mood and emotions are also affected; chronic stress is strongly related to anxiety, depression, impulsive risk taking, and aggressive behavior (Andersen & Teicher, 2008).

Perception and Stress

People respond to stressors in different ways. Your stress reactivity might increase when treated unfairly or dismissively by your principal. Another teacher might not be as bothered by the principal's behavior but may feel highly stressed when students misbehave in the classroom or when seeing a student suffer in some way. The circumstances that trigger your stress and determine its level of intensity can differ from those of others, but the underlying mechanisms are the same. At base, we *perceive* an event as threatening, and we react defensively. The brain operates as our perceiver-in-chief, making decisions about what is threatening and what is not, and allowing the rest of the system to respond accordingly (McEwen & Gianaros, 2010). Perception of threat is largely the work of the amygdala and related brain networks, and it is a process that happens rapidly, automatically, and generally without reflection (Bishop, 2008; LeDoux, 2003). Traumatic experiences, especially in early life, or chronic stress can prime the amygdala to overidentify threats in the environment. Some of the belligerence or difficulties students present in classrooms or with their peers might reflect their unconscious perception that others present some kind of threat to them. In more serious cases, this phenomenon has been called *hostile attribution bias* (Crick & Dodge, 1994), which means a persistent bias toward perceiving the world as threatening and deserving of retaliation even when the cues are ambiguous. For young adolescents who experience negative teasing on social media, neutral comments are more likely to be perceived as negative and to provoke an antagonistic response (Barnett, Nichols, Sonnentag, & Wadian, 2013).

When our brain registers something as threatening, some of the more control-based functions of the brain, like the prefrontal cortex, go off-line and operate less effectively. Remember that the stress system's job is to defend us, and it may not wait to see if the threat is a truly dangerous person or just a shadow. When a stimulus is perceived as a threat, such as a person with an ominous-looking object in hand, the stress system kicks into gear. A full-out rush of adrenaline, cortisol, and other chemical messengers prepares our bodies with sufficient resources and energy to vanquish the threat. The amygdala and other parts of the stress response system move into ascendancy, rendering the more reflective parts of the brain less functional.

This is helpful in the proper circumstances, when the threat is really a threat. But the truth is that our stress response system, evolved to respond to physiological, life-threatening events, has the same response to psychological threats. These are not threats to physical survival, but threats to survival of the psychological self. These psychological perceptions (e.g., *They think I'm a loser. I can't pass this test. Things are getting too hard for me*) can be inaccurate, ambiguous, or unknowable in the first place. Nonetheless, they can generate a good deal of stress and anxiety and cause physical changes in the body. As in the social media study mentioned above, the mind rushes to automatic, emotional explanations that can result in problematic social behavior.

How Mindfulness Buffers Stress

Teachers and students are not at their best when they are chronically stressed at school. The chances of discipline problems, bullying, aggression, and anxiety escalate while those of real learning diminish. But, as we know all too well, the stress of life is not going away, and some of it is complicated and difficult to resolve easily. What if there were a way to make us more aware of our own reactivity, so that we could be more in control? What if we could prevent some of the wear and tear on our bodies and minds that can hurt us and lead to burning out? Mindfulness practice, or the systematic cultivation of present-moment nonjudgmental attention, operates on the brain and body systems involved in the stress response system to do just that.

In studies with adults, mindfulness practice has been shown to down-regulate certain parts of the autonomic nervous system that respond to the first signs of imminent threat or stress (Hölzel, 2010). The effect of this dampening is that one's perception of stress or threat is more modulated and less intense (de Vibe, Bjørndal, Tipton, Hammerstrøm, & Kowalski, 2012). Other systems that are activated by the stress response, such as inflammatory processes, become more balanced and less prone to dysregulation (Black & Slavich, 2016). Bringing attention to present-moment experience shifts attentional focus away from the past (e.g., troubling memories) and the future (e.g., apprehension of impending events), thereby reducing the connections between automatic cognitive routines and habitual, reflexive patterns of behavior. Experience is perceived from a different perspective, with greater degrees of freedom.

SEEING WITH NEW EYES

With her arms full of school supplies, Karen walks out into another wintry day and hurries to start her car. She tries to remember the things she needs to bring with her to school. It's the week of parent conferences, so she'll have to stay late. She is dreading the long day at school, already worrying about feeling too tired to talk to all the parents who need her. Karen's road to school passes a broad expanse of open fields surrounded by low hills in the distance. She drives along the winding road, her head filled with items from her endless to-do list, and catches a glimpse of a large oak tree, its shape silhouetted against the growing lightness of the sky. It surprises her that she's never noticed this particular tree before. Its stark beauty captures her attention, and she pulls over for a brief moment to take it in. *Maybe practicing mindfulness is helping me notice some things I didn't notice before,* she thinks.

Karen can feel the tension in her shoulders relax and the tightness in her chest loosen up. Inexplicably, she notices that her frame of mind has changed a bit. Compared to her earlier trepidation about the long day ahead, she's feeling a bit more at ease after these moments of present-moment attention. She takes another minute or two to pay attention to the color of the landscape, the shape of the valley, the faraway mountains, and to her body as she sits in the stillness.

Later in the day, she recalls this experience and wonders, *What might I not be seeing in my students; what have I not noticed before? I might be surprised,* she thinks, *if I could see them with new eyes.* As they work in groups, Karen decides to experiment with observing each student mindfully, as if she's seeing them for the first time.

For children and youth, mindfulness can support both *top-down* and *bottom-up* processes that involve learning and emotion (Zelazo & Lyons, 2012). Mindfulness practice strengthens those areas of the brain, like the prefrontal cortex, that are responsible for top-down regulation. We will show how mindfulness supports these top-down functions in Chapter 3. There are also bottom-up effects. Mindfulness practice reduces the overactivity of the amygdala and related brain structures, lessening their susceptibility to constant, intense triggering by stressful events. Researchers propose that attending to internal and external events in a mindful, nonreactive way moderates the wear and tear on our bodies and minds that leads to illness and burnout (Creswell & Lindsay, 2014).

This information might help secondary teachers understand why some adolescents appear reactive, hostile, or removed. A mind under stress, just like a mind on automatic pilot, is a mind that is not ready to learn and not able to see things clearly. It's obvious from years of research that we should take stress seriously, especially if we're in the business of education (Diamond, 2013). Sometimes understanding our own stress burden is a good place to start, so consider reflecting or journaling your responses to the following questions and doing the foundational practices below.

Reflecting on This Chapter

Try journaling your responses to the following questions:

Is there a situation or a student who triggers a lot of stress in me?

What have I noticed about my mental and physical health when I am
under stress?

What have I noticed about my teaching when I am under stress?

In what ways do my students show their stress?

What are my personal ways of handling stress? Which of my stress
management strategies do I think are healthy? Which are unhealthy?

**Questions available for download and printing at
http://wwnorton.com/rd/broderick**

Begin to Practice

Practice #1: Taking a Stress Inventory

At the end of the day, take a stress assessment. Make a mental or
written inventory of any times in the day when you felt particularly
stressed. Notice if you experience anything in your body as you recall
or record these events. Is there a place in the body where stress is most
noticeable? Notice any thoughts that pop into your mind as you recall
this. Reflect on any connections you observe between your mental
stress and your body's response.

Sample:

Stressful event	Date and time of day	Were you aware of the stress when you were experiencing it? (Yes or No)	What sensations did you notice in your body when feeling stressed?

Practice #2: Relaxing Sigh

If you've done the stress inventory and paid attention to your body, you may see that stress causes tightness in your lower back, stomach, shoulders, chest, forehead, jaw or other areas of the body. In order to become more mindful of our stress and the mental habits that support it, it can be helpful to relax a bit. This short practice can be used whenever you wish, especially when you notice feeling stress in your body.

How to do it:

- Take a breath in through the nose and out through the mouth, making a soft sound or sigh as you slowly exhale.
- Take one more relaxing breath, focusing on the sound and feeling of the breath as you inhale through the nose and slowly out through the mouth with a soft sigh.
- Now try it three more times silently: Inhaling through the nose and out through the mouth in a long, slow, gentle breath.
- Take a moment to notice how your body is feeling right now.
- Later, you can do it silently whenever you become aware of tension. You can do this anywhere, but you could also practice this more intentionally by sitting in a chair with your eyes closed or letting your gaze fall softly a few feet in front of you.

How to Do the Relaxing Sigh with Your Students

If you have practiced the relaxing sigh yourself and feel comfortable with it, you can teach it to your students. Try it when seated or standing, to allow for different experiences. This practice can be used at any time in the course of the day, but it may be particularly helpful when students are unsettled or stressed, when you sense some anxiety (e.g., before a test), or before transitioning to another task. Remember to do this along with your students. In this way, you illustrate that we all need to be alert to the buildup of stress and that we can intentionally step out of automatic pilot. In practicing with them, you offer a model and means of self-care.

Tips to Take Away

Stress comes from external as well as internal events. The brain is our perceiver-in-chief, and we often react to perceived threats (stress) without awareness. The chain of physiological events that stress triggers in the mind causes wear and tear that can result in mental and physical illness over the long term. Adolescents are reactive to threats, especially in social situations, so they need to understand how their minds and bodies work if they are to take more control over their stress. Mindfulness is an antidote to stress because it alters this mental and physical cascade and reduces the wear and tear on our systems.

Attention:
The Foundation for
Teaching and Learning

Teachers know, without needing to rely on any pedagogical theory, that students must pay attention in order to learn. Our understanding may be enriched, however, by relatively recent scientific knowledge about attention, learning, and stress. Attention is the gateway to learning. We select from a large amount of data in the environment that we will process, integrate, and encode. Attention can be involuntary, as when you automatically turn your head to find the source of a loud noise in the classroom. But much of our attention is voluntary or selective. We choose to pay attention or to focus on something and ignore something else.

Recently, researchers have been very interested in attention-related mental skills. Collectively, these top-down processes are called *executive functions* (EFs) and include attention and working memory, inhibitory control, and cognitive flexibility (Blair & Diamond, 2008; Diamond, 2013; Zelazo, Blair, & Willoughby, 2017). Executive functions allow students to retain information in working memory in order to hold ideas in mind; to compare, contrast, or integrate them; to generate and test hypotheses; and to perform other important mental operations. They provide for the control that is needed to sustain attention on tasks; inhibit irrelevant information; and prevent overlearned, automatic assumptions from overriding new learning. They're also critical for reasoning and interpersonal relationships that require considering multiple perspectives or novel ways of problem solving.

Even though adolescents show greatly improved executive functioning and increased ability to monitor and reflect on their own thinking (called metacognition) compared to younger children, growth in these areas continues into adulthood. Therefore, it's important to remember that the teenage prefrontal cortex, the brain area generally associated with these skills, is still developing its capacity to hold things in mind, to resist interference, to return attention to tasks that might be tedious or require effort, and to monitor performance (Gogtay et al., 2004). Moreover, these functions are more than straightforward products of a cool and rational cognitive system. Brain networks for cognition and emotion are highly interconnected, making it impossible to address attention without considering the influence of emotional and social factors (Pessoa, 2017). Executive skills are frequently overpowered by powerful affective impulses, particularly during adolescence (Pharo, Sim, Graham, Gross, & Hayne, 2011). The teenager's propensity for impulsive decision making and risk taking, especially when peers are present, and for ruminative brooding, reflect common shortcomings of underdeveloped executive control systems. More serious executive function difficulties are associated with diagnoses like ADHD and other learning and emotional problems of adolescents (Kittel, Schmidt, & Hilbert, 2017; Leno et al., 2017) but adolescents' brains, on the whole, are still under development during this period.

MOVING FROM THEORY TO PRACTICE
The Importance of Evidence

Although these are exciting times for mindfulness in education, we still have a lot to learn about the best and most effective applications for children and youth. This book emphasizes what we do know from the available research findings, arguably not always perceived as the most useful tools for practitioners. However, the growing movement toward accountability for professionals makes it important for teachers and others to choose and implement practices and programs that have evidence to support them and that do no harm. As you've read, most of the research on the effectiveness of mindfulness has been done with adults and shows that mindfulness is *as effective or even more effective* than many conventional treatments for pain, depression, anxiety, smoking, and addictions (Goldberg et al., 2018). As exciting as this is, it's important not to overpromise benefits for youth, like higher SAT scores. Keep in mind that the evidence base is still being built. Currently, analyses of studies in schools show positive effects, especially on some cognitive and stress-related measures, but more studies are needed to examine longer term outcomes like increased academic success and improved social relationships. A meta-analysis by Carsley and colleagues (Carsley et al., 2018) found that the greatest mental health improvements were observed for students who were most at risk and for students in later adolescence (ages 15–18).

Science has a formal way to investigate problems and draw conclusions about outcomes using statistical and other methods. Questions such as "Does this program work?" are subjected to a rigorous process so that conclusions can be as free from personal bias as possible. When evidence is aggregated, such as in meta-analyses that report results from multiple studies, the evidence can be particularly significant. As with any scientific endeavor, knowledge builds relatively slowly and is buttressed by repeated observations of similar results. Sometimes, based on our own preferences or personal experience, we have expectations that an educational practice or a program works. However, this is not sufficient to justify its use from a scientific standpoint. When educators want to commit time and resources to programs or practices, it's ethical to consider the best evidence available. Decisions based on evidence can benefit from the rigorous safeguards built into the research process. These safeguards make research outcomes more likely to be correct when compared to many other methods of proof.

Not all evidence is equally valid. Educators should be cautious about the sources of information they accept before making decisions about classroom practices. Scientific researchers are required to follow ethical guidelines in conducting and reporting research. Testimonials from satisfied customers of commercial ventures certainly may be helpful, but they cannot be considered research evidence. Remember that testimonials don't always include participants who fail to provide glowing reviews. The best way to see scientific evidence is in peer-reviewed publications. The review process guarantees that others, not just program developers, have examined the evidence objectively and without compensation. Being an informed consumer is an important way for teachers to exercise responsibility in decision making about social and emotional learning practices and programs in their classrooms.

As you might recall from your own life, perhaps during a period of personal challenge, stress impairs mental skills. Stress can limit the capacity of working memory, undermine task performance, and orient attention to threatening cues (Liston, McEwen, Casey, & Posner, 2009; Moran, 2016). These effects can be observed not only in the wake of major trauma but also when stress is short term or routine. Importantly for teachers, degraded executive functioning can be an early warning signal of student stress because the learning brain is an emotional brain. As Diamond so powerfully describes,

> Executive functions (EF) and prefrontal cortex are the first to suffer, and suffer disproportionately, if something is not right in your life. They suffer first, and most, if you are <u>stressed</u>, <u>sad</u>, <u>lonely</u>, <u>sleep deprived</u> or <u>not physically fit</u>. Any of these can cause you to appear to have a disorder of EFs, such as ADHD, when you do not. You can see the deleterious effects of stress, sadness, loneliness, and lack of physical health or fitness at the physiological and neuroanatomical level in prefrontal cortex and at the behavioral level in worse EFs (poorer reasoning and problem-solving, forgetting things, and impaired ability to exercise discipline and self-control). If we want schoolchildren, workers, or business executives to have better attention and concentration, be better able to reason and problem solve, we cannot ignore stresses in their lives. (2013, p. 153–154)

Every year, the American Psychological Association (APA) surveys Americans about their stress. In 2014, the APA included teens in its large online assessment (APA, 2014). The results were a wake-up call. Teens reported higher overall stress levels than adults (5.8 versus 5.1 on a 10-point scale). For 83% of adolescents, school was a notable source of stress. Teens reported feeling unprepared to handle stress and engaged in many unproductive coping behaviors like procrastination, overeating or skipping meals, surfing the web, playing video games, and watching TV. Those with high levels of stress reported feeling depressed, overwhelmed, sleep-deprived, angry, and irritable. Perhaps unsurprisingly, highly stressed adults reported similar symptoms and similar coping mechanisms. More recent surveys (APA, 2017) did not include teenagers but demonstrated that millennials (i.e., the group born between 1982–2000) had the highest levels of stress (5.7 out of 10) compared to other age groups studied. This latter survey also took a close look at the relationship between stress and technology use, finding that millennials were more concerned than other age groups about the effects of technology on their mental and physical health. Survey respondents who identified as "constant checkers" of online media had higher stress levels overall than "nonconstant" checkers.

We can't avoid stress, and some level of physiological arousal is necessary for attention and performance or we would all fall asleep (Yerkes & Dodson, 1908). However, chronically elevated levels of aversive stress, like those reported in the surveys above, can reduce the effectiveness of executive functions that are needed to succeed in school (McEwen, 2016; Moran, 2016). Furthermore, stress compromises the ability to revise existing ideas by updating them with new information, which is the essential characteristic of learning. It also limits the flexibility of higher order cognitive skills that are tapped by measures of achievement at the secondary school level. Compounding the problem, we actually do remember stressful experiences, like social exclusion or school failure, very well. Stressful events can be firmly encoded in memory, often shaping our long-term anxieties about ourselves and our abilities (Vogel & Schwabe, 2016).

Certainly, the high stress levels youth report are not all related to technology. But, in this chapter on attention, we should recognize the power technologies have to devour our time and fragment our attention. Some researchers have gone so far as to explain our common difficulties with staying organized and managing time with living in a highly stimulating environment that constantly draws our attention off task. The results are a low but chronic level of anxiety called attention deficit trait (see Hallowell & Ratey, 2005). Many students appear to be attached to their devices, solitary even while connected to the online world at their fingertips. Some research in this area suggests that there is something unique and problematic about screen use (Twenge, Joiner, Rogers, & Martin, 2017). Perhaps it reduces feelings of belongingness and emotional connection that are supported by in-person interaction. Teenagers who spend more time on screen activities are significantly more likely to report depressive symptoms and suicide-related behavior, greater loneliness, higher levels of obesity, more sleep problems, cyberbullying, and academic problems than adolescents who spend more time on non-screen activities, like homework; reading print media; in-person social interaction, athletics, and attending religious services. In some ways, rapidly changing technology mirrors the accelerating pace of life that affects not only adults but younger and younger generations. The virtual world offers an illusory escape from the competing demands of school, work, family, and peers, but it can degrade the quality of attention needed for success in school. Is there an antidote to the problem of fragmented attention?

Training Attention

Conventional thinking about attention has viewed it as a relatively fixed individual characteristic. We might assess one student as very attentive and another as having a poor attention span. Approaching attention with a fixed mindset, however, is constraining and differs substantially from current evidence that suggests attention is malleable. So much of what is covered in this book owes a debt to neuroscience, the field that teaches us that the brain and its workings are trainable. In fact, the brain is the one organ designed to change as a function of experience (Doidge, 2007). As you have read, mindfulness is a particular kind of attention, so its practice might have something to add to the basic toolkit students need in any classroom.

Research with youth and young adults has been encouraging about the possibility for improving executive functions through mindfulness practice. Improvements in attention and other cognitive skills have been documented for regular education students and those with attention problems after mindfulness training (Maynard, Solis, Miller, & Brendel, 2017; Zylowska et al., 2008). Some research shows that mindfulness practice improved working memory skills and reduced mind wandering for college students, as reflected on their GRE exam scores (Mrazek, Franklin, Phillips, Baird, & Schooler, 2013). High school students who had participated in a structured mindfulness program showed significant improvements on computerized tests of certain executive functions compared to students who did not participate (Frank et al., manuscript in preparation). Although more research needs to be done, the existing evidence shows promise.

LEARNING ABOUT ATTENTION

Darryl has noticed that his 6th period class has been off task recently. Some of the students are nodding off and others just seem more jittery than usual. He's been hearing more complaints from students about being stressed out and having too much to do in his class.

I just can't pay attention with all the noise in the building, says one student.

I keep thinking about what I have to do after school, says another.

It's too hard, says a third.

Darryl has taught his class some simple practices like deep breathing to help students relieve their stress. He decides to give them an opportunity to practice mindfulness as well. He tells them:

Attention is skill we can develop, just as we develop physical strength and stamina. But, just as in athletics, we have to practice. Let's practice paying attention to something we do every day—eating.

Some students are confused.

How is eating something going to help me in school?

Darryl explains how attention is the foundation for success and that it is a skill that can be trained by paying attention to everyday things.

If you are able to tune in and notice where your attention is, you

can also notice when you get distracted. Then, with some practice,
you can get better at returning attention to what you're doing. You
can strengthen your attention so that you can focus a little better.

The students seem willing to give it a try. Darryl hands out a
single raisin to each student and guides them through the process
of eating mindfully. Afterward, Darryl asks:

What did you notice?

Each student has a different response.

I never ate a raisin like that before. I thought I liked them but I
really didn't like this at all. I hate raisins.

I usually just eat them in bunches without thinking . . . that's the
way I usually eat and I don't really taste them. It's kind of weird to
really taste something.

Yeah, I sort of feel full just after eating one raisin. I guess I never
really paid attention before.

A foundational mindfulness practice, awareness of breath, is generally
considered a practice that trains attentional focus because attention is centered on the breath in the body. Let's explore how this basic mindfulness
practice relates to executive functions.

In practicing awareness of breath, you are invited to bring your attention to your breath and notice any accompanying sensations in your body.
This step engages basic executive skills of orienting attention to a partic-

ular object of focus (breathing) and maintains attention on the breath as continuously as possible (*working memory*). Mind wandering is noted, and attention is intentionally returned to its focus on the breath (*inhibition of distraction*). Distractions may routinely capture attention, especially when starting to practice, but practice in focusing *on purpose* strengthens the ability to recognize and inhibit them. When attention is returned to the breath after recognizing distractions, it is done with gentleness and flexibility (*cognitive flexibility*). One particular attitude of mindful practice, nonjudgment, fosters observation of these mental processes without need for evaluation or mental commentary. Any tendency to give up, get discouraged, or engage in self-criticism or other self-defeating action is modulated by a compassion stance toward our own distractible, fragmented, and all-too-human mind. We gently return attention to breathing upon noticing our distraction, making this in itself a moment of mindful awareness. The fact that many distractions exist during a practice period does not mean that practice is not helpful. It is simply what happened at that time. Thus, one's nonreactivity or dispassionate observation of the experience—whatever it happens to be—also strengthens emotion regulation skills such as recognizing and accepting emotions, persisting in our effort, and modulating emotional reactivity (see Lutz, Slagter, Dunne, & Davidson, 2008, and Chapter 5). The executive functions of working memory, inhibiting distractions, flexible shifting of attention, and emotion regulation are all cultivated in this simple breath-awareness practice.

It is strongly recommended that teachers practice awareness of breath themselves before introducing it to students. Mindfulness has been called a *practice* because it is a type of procedural knowledge (Broderick & Frank, 2014). Most academic teaching relies on transmitting another type of knowledge, called *declarative*. Declarative knowledge answers "what" questions and is composed of a body of facts and information. It can be taught in directive ways because teachers are experts in particular information domains. *Nondeclarative* procedural knowledge answers the question "how." Without personal experience of mindfulness practice, teaching resembles that of a swimming instructor who never got into the water. If teachers have not experienced the "how," it's more difficult to teach it to others.

A NEW KIND OF HOMEWORK

Julie was thrilled to get her first job in a middle school. She spent a lot of her summer preparing and revising some lessons she'd found useful during her field experience. She felt some nervous anticipation, but she told herself that this was to be expected. New teachers had a lot to learn, and things would go smoothly after she had more experience. Teaching in a real job, however, turns out to be harder than she'd expected. Her students sense she is unsure of herself, and they start to take advantage of her. Every day she feels she has more, rather than fewer, experiences of feeling out of control. She is starting to worry if teaching is the right career for her. During her internship, Julie's supervising teacher had introduced the class to mindfulness. Back then, she had practiced it herself, and it helped her cope while she was getting certified. She thinks it might help her now. Julie decides to get up 15 minutes earlier in the morning to practice. Over time, she becomes better at sensing the anxiety that wells up within her when students try to test her authority. More often than before, she holds her ground, and focuses on her breath as a way of restoring balance. Even though it's still hard, she is able to return her attention to her lesson without getting swept away by other concerns. Gradually, her students test limits less frequently, and she starts to feel more confident.

Some mindfulness practices are considered *formal*, which means that they follow a particular sequence and may be done on a regular basis (e.g., every morning) while others are called *informal*. Informal practice is the practice of mindfulness in daily life, on the spot. Generally, formal practices provide the foundation and the experiential knowledge of mindfulness that practitioners can use to generalize to everyday situations.

Before guiding formal mindfulness practice in the classroom, teachers should give some thought to the physical surroundings. It can be extremely helpful to provide a space for practice that is different from the regular classroom, because classrooms can be associated with anxiety and demands for performance, especially for some students. Clearly, this will be neither possible nor efficient for many teachers to manage, so adjusting the space you have may be a better option. Consider moving chairs into a circle or adjusting seating so that students have space to sit comfortably without being too close to one another. If possible, dim the lights to reduce overhead glare, or provide for alternative lighting. Some teachers may wish to use string lights to soften the light in the classroom.

Adding a short period of movement or stretching can help students transition to greater stillness from the busyness or tension buildup they feel after sitting still for long periods of time. A loud or disorganized classroom will work against students' attempts to focus attention, so it's important to take time to set the stage. Use of a soothing sound, like a bell or a chime, can be a cue for the start of practice. Keep the practice periods short, especially at the beginning. Prepare adolescents for their first exposure to formal mindfulness practice by offering some rationale for the practice and by inviting them to participate. If adolescents choose not to practice, there's not much any adult can or should do, for this is something that should not be forced. However, students who choose not to participate should avoid disturbing others. Establishing some guidelines, preferably through group discussion and consensus, can be helpful before beginning.

What follows are suggestions for short practices and other ways to strengthening attention in a mindful way. The formal breath awareness practice found at the end of this chapter is the foundation for all these suggestions.

Short Mindfulness Practices Based on Awareness of Breath

TAKING THREE MINDFUL BREATHS

Once you are familiar with the basic awareness of breath practice, try taking three mindful breaths multiple times each day. You might decide to use a certain place as a reminder for this practice or set a timer for a particular time of day. For example, teachers can practice this before or after class. Students can practice when they are in a certain place (e.g., standing in front of their lockers) or at a specific time (e.g. before they start their homework). This short script for three breaths can be used after you have practiced the longer one at the end of the chapter.

Take a moment to let go of any thoughts or preoccupations that are in your mind right now and feel the breath in your body. Just notice the breath wherever it's easiest for you to do so. Bring your full attention to the breath, and let it follow the in-breath and the out-breath as best you can. Notice the sensations of breathing and any thoughts or feelings that come up. Pay mindful attention for three full breaths.

THREE DOTS

This is another way to remember to take three mindful breaths during the day. Give each student three dot stickers and invite them to put the stickers in three places they routinely see during the day (e.g., a bathroom mirror; a cell phone or computer; the inside of a locker door). Each time they see the dots, invite them to take three mindful breaths.

MY DAILY DOSE OF MINDFULNESS

Another way to practice mindfulness is to focus your awareness fully on one thing. Choose an activity to do mindfully and make it a daily practice. It could be something like brushing your teeth, walking up a certain stairway, or preparing a meal or a snack.

MINDFUL TRANSITIONS

The normal transitions that occur at school: beginnings, endings, moving into groups, or starting a new task, can become opportunities for practicing mindful awareness. Allow for some silence as you take a few mindful breaths, inviting students to be more intentional about their work and the choices they make.

Remember that even tiny moments of awareness should be celebrated. Take one small moment, whenever you wish during the day, and begin.

Reflecting on This Chapter

Try journaling your responses to the following questions:

How do I view attention? Is it fixed or malleable? Has my view altered after reading this chapter? How might this information affect my teaching?

How might my students respond to practicing mindfulness in the classroom?

What concerns do I have about bringing mindfulness to my students or school?

Choose an activity of daily life for your own practice. What is it? What can you do to help yourself remember to practice?

Questions available for download and printing at
http://wwnorton.com/rd/broderick

Begin to Practice

Practice #1: Awareness of Breath

Take some time to offer suggestions before starting to practice. Ask students to put down whatever they're holding, turn off cell phones, and find an upright but comfortable position in their chairs: feet flat on the floor, hands resting in lap, back straight but not stiff. Invite students to close their eyes, if that is comfortable for them; otherwise, direct them to let their gaze fall softly a few feet in front of them. If students are restless, start with some movement (e.g., standing stretches) before sitting down to practice. Dim the lights if possible. If students feel uncomfortable with the novelty of sitting in silence, you could also have them turn their chairs around to face the walls, so that they are less self-conscious. Wait until the class settles and then begin, using the script below. Guide the practice slowly with appropriate pauses.

Please find a comfortable position with your feet flat on the floor, your back straight but not too stiff, and your hands resting comfortably in your lap. Allow your facial muscles to relax. If you feel comfortable, allow your eyes to close or let your gaze fall softly in front of you. We'll be spending these next few minutes practicing mindful attention to the breath, following your breath as it moves in and out of the nostrils.

. . . Let's start by becoming aware of the breath.

. . . Notice your breath wherever it's easiest for you:
Moving in and out at the nostrils,
Perhaps at the chest,
Or maybe at the belly.

. . . Letting your breath move in and out at its own pace.

. . . Just feeling your breath, and letting your attention follow it from the beginning of the in-breath to the end of the out-breath.

. . . If you wish, place your hand on your belly and feel the movement of your breath, whatever that is like for you right now.

. . . And if your mind wanders, that's not a problem. Just bring your attention back to the breath whenever you notice it has drifted away.

. . . We're just focusing on one thing right now: following the breath with full attention and interest, and without changing anything.

. . . We're mindfully paying attention to what's inside.

. . . Simply allow yourself to rest your attention on the breath for a few more cycles.

At the conclusion of the practice, gently invite students to open their eyes when they're ready and return their attention to the classroom. You may ring a soft bell to conclude, if you wish.

Practice #2: Mindful Media Use

Experiment with texting or emailing mindfully as your practice. You might wish to try this in class by sending a text or email, or by copying the steps for the students to practice at home. The practice can be adapted for many different kinds of media use.

Please find a comfortable position with your feet flat on the floor, your back straight but not too stiff, and your hands resting comfortably in your lap. Allow your facial muscles to relax. We'll be spending these next few minutes practicing mindful attention.
Let's start by becoming aware of the breath as it moves in your body.

. . . Pick up your phone, hold it in your hand, and notice its shape, size, and weight.

. . . Explore any feelings you might notice right now,

. . . Feelings of anxiousness,

. . . Anticipation,

. . . Any restlessness or urge to move that may be present in your body and mind.

. . . Just try to become aware of any urge to open the message. What does this feel like for you?

. . . Now, more slowly than you usually do, feel the movement of your hand as you raise it to touch the screen. Feel the contact with the screen as you click to open the message.

. . . Bring your attention to your breath in your body as you see the message. Notice if there are any changes in your breath. Are there any thoughts you can notice? Any feelings?

. . . Begin reading the message. Notice the quality of your attention (impatient, slow, deliberate, distracted, scattered, etc.). Notice if this is different from the way you normally use social media; notice if the quality of your attention is different.

Tips to Take Away

Executive functions related to attention include working memory, inhibiting distractions, and flexible cognitive shifting. The quality of attention is related to these top-down as well as bottom-up affective processes. In adolescence, social and emotional influences and the use of technology may affect adolescents' attention quality and their performance. EFs continue to develop into adulthood and may be strengthened by mindfulness practice. The basic mindfulness of breath practice can support executive functions and emotion regulation skills by reducing interference in working memory, shifting attention, and exercising regulation of mental processes.

Motivation and Engagement: The Contribution of Mindful Interest

Boredom and restlessness are common complaints of adolescents, ones they frequently associate with schoolwork and other academic activities. Given the reward-seeking adolescent brain, physiologically primed for excitement and oriented toward social interactions (Casey, 2015; Casey, Jones, & Somerville, 2011), this is no surprise. Teachers take the issue of student motivation seriously, especially because academic motivation declines during the adolescent period (Eccles, Wigfield, & Schiefele, 1998; Finn, 1989). Training programs for educators routinely address ways to increase the relevance of classroom lessons and to provide strategies for incorporating developmental needs into instruction. Some adolescent-friendly tools include allowing for reasonable autonomy; fostering effort attributions; and creating caring, respectful relationships within a safe school space. There is no doubt that relevance, respect, caring, safety, and effort are well-established motivational principles and that teachers routinely enact them in their classrooms to the benefit of students, especially those most at risk (Christenson, Reschly, & Wylie, 2012).

One simple way to dichotomize motivation is to distinguish between extrinsic and intrinsic types (Deci, 1975). In elementary school, the use of food, points, or prizes (i.e., extrinsic rewards) are popular ways of motivating students to act in certain ways. But by middle and high school, many of those extrinsic rewards have lost at least some of their power. This may explain why strategies for adolescents privilege more autonomy-granting and relationship-based interventions.

One motivational approach that has been successful, especially for students with a history of school failure, involves challenging student assumptions about their fundamental ability to learn (Dweck, 2017; Yeager & Dweck, 2012). Dweck's work on *mindset* delineates two sets of achievement-related assumptions characteristic of those who are energized by challenges and those who are more likely to give up. She explains that belief in the malleability of basic intelligence undergirds a growth mindset, primed for effort and persistence in the face of difficulty. Its opposite, a fixed mindset, holds that basic ability is a predetermined quantity, and that efforts to improve it are doomed to failure. Growth mindset interventions involve recognizing and challenging beliefs about the immutability of intelligence. As you recall, the brain is trainable, and the effects of environmental expe-

MOVING FROM THEORY TO PRACTICE
The Importance of Prevention

Mindfulness in education is part of the SEL approach to student wellness that takes a preventive focus. Some programs in schools are targeted to those students who show symptoms of learning or emotional problems and who are most at risk. In contrast to *targeted* programs in schools that may involve pulling students out of class, *universal* prevention is offered to all students as part of their regular programming. It is intended to promote long-term success and to intervene before problems become established and harder to treat. Universal prevention is not intended to replace more targeted intervention but rather to supplement it. Prevention has far-reaching benefits not only for public health but also for the economy. A benefit-cost analysis was done by researchers from Columbia University to calculate the long-term economic outcomes of SEL prevention programs (Belfield et al., 2015). Analysis of six well-established programs showed benefits to participants that exceeded program costs in terms of future earnings, educational level, and reduced need for social supports. For every dollar invested in these aggregated SEL interventions, there was an $11 return on investment. A preventive focus makes sense in schools because these settings provide access to a wide audience and potentially offer benefits at the lowest cost, especially for youth who might not otherwise receive mental health information and support.

Taking a prevention focus requires trust. Adolescents in schools, unlike adults in mindfulness classes, are non-volunteers. When mindfulness is offered as part of the regular curriculum, the level of interest and engagement will vary. Since mindfulness is fundamentally an internal process, effects may be subtle. Therefore, we shouldn't make categorical interpretations of students' mental states. Neither should we draw premature conclusions about the acceptability of mindfulness programs for youth. Adolescents' mental states are a mystery to most adults, and it's not possible to know what they are absorbing because they may not want to tell us, and the fruits of intervention may not have fully ripened (Bailey, Chambers, Wootten, & Hassed, 2018).

---

rience literally operate to change physiological systems even at the level of genes (Meaney, 2010). So, providing students with this information about the ways their brains operate can be tremendously helpful in supporting belief in their potential and in activating their efforts to learn.

Many of the motivational approaches in use, however, are teacher-directed efforts that modify classroom routines, instruction, and interactions. This is only part of the story. As with learning itself, motivation is not solely due to extrinsic circumstances or conditions. Motivation is also an inside job. Mindset interventions that help students understand the role of their beliefs offer one student-centered alternative. They provide knowledge about the brain and some self-talk strategies to use when dysfunctional thoughts arise. As such, they invite students to take personal responsibility for their learning, potentially reducing reliance on teachers as external sources of motivation. Mindfulness offers yet another step toward intrinsic motivation because it cultivates key internal building blocks that support learning. It does this, not primarily through provision of declarative knowledge or guidelines for challenging unhelpful beliefs, but rather through the *first-person experiential practice of interest.*

Interest

Although there is some current discussion among researchers about the nature of interest, many say its importance has been overlooked (Silvia, 2008). Interest is significant for a number of reasons but primarily because it is deeply connected to more overtly cognitive capacities like attention, intelligence, persistence, and goal-directed behavior (Ainley, 2012; O'Keefe & Harackiewicz, 2017). Interest sits on the border between cognition and emotion, sharing features from both camps (Tracy & Randles, 2011). It can be construed as a state of attention *and* an emotion because attention is sustained by the positive feelings associated with the interesting object or experience.

Early emotion researchers partitioned basic emotions (e.g., innate and universal) into positive and negative varieties that motivate us to act in particular ways (Frijda & Parrott, 2011; Izard, 2011). Emotions can propel us toward something (e.g., affiliation with others) or have us move away (e.g., avoidance of threat). As a basic human tendency, interest has been associated with seeking, attending, and acquiring information (moving toward) while lack of interest is associated with its opposite (moving away). In Izard's classic interpretation of basic emotions (1971), interest held a preeminent place in the group of basic emotions we are equipped with at birth. Our basic set of emotional building blocks is slanted toward the more negative pole (i.e., anger, sadness, fear, and disgust) while interest and joy reflect innate capacities on the positive side of the scale. Izard viewed interest as the *driver of selective attention*, the primary emotion that drives all subsequent processing of information.

Regardless of theoretical arguments about the nature of emotions, there is agreement that interest is a fundamental human capacity and a positive resource for flourishing. Interested people have greater resilience, and the emotion of interest is tied to intrinsic motivation, curiosity, exploration, and seeking information (Fredrickson, 1998; Izard & Ackerman, 2000). It is also related to improvements in learning and memory (Kang et al., 2009) and the pursuit of greater meaningfulness in life (Kashdan & Steger, 2007). Flum and Kaplan (2006) note that the level of adolescent exploratory, inquisitive thinking is correlated with greater cognitive flexibility, tolerance of ambiguity, and perception of situations as challenges rather than problems. Thus, interest may be a component of a growth mindset.

Cultivating Interest

Consider this example. I am inherently motivated to learn about or accomplish A, because A is interesting to me, and I like it. On the other hand, B does not interest me, nor do I like it. Therefore, I am less motivated (or even completely unmotivated) to engage with B. Sadly, the B category may describe the whole of schooling for some adolescents, and this might be due to prior experiences with school failure.

You might be thinking that trying to interest certain students in certain tasks is a futile enterprise. This may be so, because no motivational system comes with a 100% guarantee. Just as we might think about intelligence and attention capacity, however, we frequently assume that we have a relatively limited range of things that are of interest to us. Consequently, interest is viewed as a fixed quantity. But interest is a basic and renewable human resource that is associated with life-long learning and well-being.

MY INTERESTING MIND

Luis likes to practice mindfulness with his class on a regular basis. Today, he's going to lead the class in a body scan, a practice they have done several times before. Before they start, Luis asks them to be aware of their thoughts, the mental chatter that they notice as they practice. After they finish, some students comment on their experience. Some notice increased ability to focus and more patience. Some report more restlessness:

I was thinking—this is so slow. It's giving me a headache to try to focus my mind on my breath.

I was thinking about homework, and I couldn't get my thoughts to stop.

I never knew there was so much stuff going on inside my head.

Luis models curiosity and nonjudgment:

That's good noticing! Isn't it interesting that our minds are filled with so many thoughts? They just come and go on their own, and this is something that happens to everyone. We all noticed something different, even if it wasn't relaxing or pleasant. We're all learning a little more about how minds work, no matter what our own particular experience is. When we see how the mind chatters, we can learn to gently let go of random thoughts and refocus.

Luis allows the students a few more minutes to practice noticing their thoughts and then letting them go as best they can.

One student says, *This helps me because I don't have to worry about every thought being really serious. My head doesn't hurt as much.*

Yeah, says another, *I learned I have a jittery mind, but that everyone else's mind is like that, too.*

Neuroscience demonstrates that mental habits can be practiced, and with practice, they can expand (Begley, 2007). What if we challenged our fixed belief that interest is a finite capacity only restricted to certain topics? What if interest were a quality of mind and heart that could be practiced? What if the underlying mental attitudes that support interest, namely open-mindedness, curiosity, and nonjudgment, could be cultivated? What if curiosity could be enhanced by being curious? These are some reasons for practicing mindfulness.

The whole process of paying attention without judging means being curious without knowing or predetermining any outcome. The mindful approach to experience is basically a scientific one, in that we keep an open mind (and heart) no matter what arises. An openhearted curiosity allows us to become trained observers of our own lived experience. Recall your practice of breath awareness from Chapter 3. It's likely that, on some occasions, your attention was stable, and your breath was regular and smooth. At other times, you might have been treated to an experience of distractibility as your mind raced around without stopping. However, the whole array of possible outcomes was met with the same basic attitude: interest. As the practice teaches: just be curious; explore the experience; and notice your thoughts, feelings, and bodily sensations.

Cultivating Interest

Adolescence is a time for self-discovery and for the growth of metacognition. Mindful self-awareness practices seem perfectly timed for youth at this stage of their development because of these emerging capacities. Many adolescents are intrigued by the concept of exploring their "inner space" as a complement to the "outer" exploration of facts, ideas, and social connections afforded them in typical secondary settings. When mindfulness practice is understood as relevant and experienced as useful, student interest and motivation can increase. Mindful attention to what's happening both on the inside and the outside, above all, can support young people's burgeoning sense of self-possession and self-regulation in the context of their natural push toward autonomy.

It's worthwhile to emphasize that the kind of noticing practiced here is called nonjudgmental (or curious). In suspending evaluation and simply exploring, we interrupt the tendency to evaluate something on automatic pilot (e.g., *I hate this* or *I love that*). This might be especially important for adolescents to understand. Imagine you're convinced you don't like something or someone. Without awareness, you might shut down and turn away. Noticing with nonjudgment does not mean that we will ultimately like or tolerate everything. It just helps to loosen the grip of implicit assumptions that keep us from thinking and acting in more creative and flexible ways.

Mindfulness practice is not intended to permit unregulated, impulsive, harmful behavior because it is about "not judging." In fact, it's quite the opposite. Mindful attention helps us to make more informed, wiser judgments about how to respond to experience. We become more aware of all the dimensions of our experience, we suspend our automatic biases, and we become less inclined to react in harmful ways. What are some potentially wiser judgments? Once we see the effects of stress on ourselves, we may conclude that letting our stress get the best of us is not helpful. This is a considered judgment. Once we investigate the transient nature of our thoughts, we may conclude that thoughts are "just thoughts." This is another judgment borne out of personal observation. Seeing for ourselves, without automatic biases, allows us to discern and act in ways that serve us well and avoid harm to others.

A mindful first-person phenomenological approach that emphasizes present-moment "knowing" rather than "knowing about" can offer a useful complement to methods of classroom learning that involve discussion of abstract concepts or rote learning. Burggraf and Grossenbacher (2008) describe a technique called *contemplative observation* that integrates first-person investigation into traditional analytic assignments. These authors describe the following project to illustrate how mindfulness can stimulate curiosity and add a deeper dimension to academic work. In addition to requiring students to write about social roles (like being a teenager and a student) from an analytic perspective, they also asked students to observe and chronicle their moment-to-moment first-person experience in each of these roles for one brief episode. The final assignment required students to compare and contrast what they learned from both third-person and first-person investigations, a process that added to the richness of the eventual product. It's possible to integrate this kind of first-person exploration into many subject area assignments, such as science, literature, social studies, art, and health, to name a few.

CURIOUSER AND CURIOUSER

Sofia finishes her lesson on how different forms of government operate across the world and how they exercise their power. She directs her students to complete a worksheet about the topic. She hears them start to mumble and asks them to explain why.

Do we have to write again? Writing about other countries is so boring.

Sofia is aware of her own impatience, but she tries to listen to what the students are telling her. She recalls the instructions she gives students when they practice mindfulness of breath every morning:

It sounds as if you're saying you're not interested. You think writing about this topic is boring. Does anyone remember how we practice interest when we do our mindfulness practice every day?

Yes, a student responds, *we're supposed to be curious about what's going on.*

Right, Sofia agrees. *Sometimes when we make up our minds that something is boring, we don't give ourselves a chance. Let's see if we can practice some curiosity about this subject, just like we do with the breath. So, instead of writing, let's draw an image of something that you remember about the lesson. It could be a cartoon image or even a word that stands out.*

As students begin to sketch, Sofia continues:

Let's consider something. Maybe you selected a certain thing to sketch because you have a tiny bit of interest in a specific country or its kind of government. As you draw, can you think of any questions you still have about the lesson? Write one or two questions next to your word or drawing.

One student offers, *I thought that monarchies were a little interesting. I was wondering how the king gets paid.*

Do people who live in socialist countries get to pick their jobs? asks another.

Sofia responds to their questions and reminds them that they are developing their capacity for interest and curiosity along with their knowledge of the lesson.

Interest can be rooted in everyday life because there's always something to take interest in. In a structured mindfulness curriculum for adolescents (Broderick, 2013), students are invited to wander around a familiar inside or outside space until they notice something they hadn't noticed before. This could be a mundane object like a cobweb in a corner or a student art project in a hallway. After mindfully observing this "event," they draw a sketch of it, which they later share with the group. They report on the unique details they observed as a result of taking a curious stance. Students could also be asked to generate as many questions as possible that emerge from this observation (e.g., *How do cobwebs form? Are there different shapes? What did the artist have in mind?*).

A fundamental characteristic of mindfulness practice is, "Be curious, and find out for yourself." Interest can be supported by teachers' encouragement to look deeply or consider something from the perspective of its sensory qualities (e.g., shape, sound, color, weight, texture). Teachers can also model an attitude of curiosity, or its opposite, in their use of questions, in the kinds of thinking they value, in their ability to notice and capitalize on student interest, and in their approach to students as individuals. It's not uncommon for teachers to feel threatened by student questions that may challenge the "right" answers or raise complicated and controversial issues in the classroom. Compassionately recognizing one's automatic assumption that a student intends to stir up trouble but not acting upon the assumption can open up more degrees of freedom for responding. Authentic curiosity (e.g., *That's a really interesting perspective. Tell us more about that*) even when needing to assert some limitations on the discussion (e.g., *That's a very interesting issue that I haven't thought about before. I'd like to take some time to think about it, so let's discuss this later*) are possibilities for more mindful inquiry.

Bear in mind that interest is a positive human resource that is associated with the kinds of cognitive and emotional skills we want to support in our students. Interest facilitates an open-mindedness that moves students' thinking from "*I can't do this*" or "*I'm not interested in this*" to "*Let's see.*" When teachers become aware of their tendency to overfocus on task completion, they can reduce their time urgency and allow for more curious exploration (e.g., *I'm feeling rushed right now, and I'm noticing some tension in my shoulders. Is anyone else noticing any tension?*).

Shifting from an exclusive *pedagogy of information* toward a *pedagogy of curiosity* (Broderick et al., 2018) can help create the context for greater student engagement. When transmission of information is the primary goal, teaching may involve lengthy analytical or didactic portions. Pressure for performance manifests in a highly goal-oriented and driven teaching style. Students may then perceive teachers as rushed, impatient, or harried. When the atmosphere is overly task-oriented, students who don't conform to the demands of the lesson may be managed using control-oriented strategies.

Alternatively, the teacher can model curiosity and a sense of wonder for students in a way that helps them internalize a curious attitude as it applies to their own life experience. A willingness to suspend automatic judgment about correctness or incorrectness of any experience while simply taking a fresh look at situations becomes possible. As Burggraf and Grossenbacher observe,

> What lies at the heart of all contemplative modes of inquiry is a direct intimate encounter with the subject matter shorn of opinion and expectation. Contemplative methods cultivate states of mind that are receptive, relaxed, ready, and even playful: the level of engagement with academic tasks (e.g., studying, writing) is therefore deep and affectively charged with motivation, and even awe. (2008, p. 4)

Reflecting on This Chapter

Try journaling your responses to the following questions:

What kinds of events or experiences am I interested in? Not interested in?

What is the quality of experience that accompanies my interest and my lack of interest? Is it pleasant, unpleasant, or neutral (give some examples).

What is my particular way of approaching things that are not interesting to me?

How do I usually try to support student interest (e.g., through intrinsic or extrinsic methods?). To what degree are these ways effective?

What would change if I altered my mindset to consider interest a trainable skill rather than a fixed quantity?

**Questions available for download and printing at
http://wwnorton.com/rd/broderick**

Begin to Practice

Practice #1: Short, Seated Body Scan

The body is a good place to start when practicing mindful curiosity. While the mind might be in the future or the past, the body is always present. Remember that this practice is not about feeling any certain way (e.g., more relaxed), but it's about paying curious and openhearted attention to what's happening in my body, right now. After providing initial guidelines for posture, eye gaze, and so on, lead the practice slowly and mindfully. Try "doing" the practice as you guide it so that you gauge the pace and the pausing based on your own experience. This allows enough time for students to connect their attention to each region of the body as they engage in curious exploration. (Before beginning, refer to the general guidelines for preparation in Chapter 3.)

> . . . *Please find a comfortable position, putting both feet flat on the floor. Your back should be straight but not too stiff, and both hands relaxed in your lap.*

> . . . *Now, become aware of your breathing.*

> . . . *Finding the breath in the body, wherever you notice it most clearly, letting your attention rest on the in-breath and the out-breath for a few breaths.*

> . . . *Then, on the next out-breath, gently guide your attention all the way down your body to the soles of both feet.*

> . . . *Allowing your attention to rest on the sensations of contact that your feet make with the solid floor.*

> . . . *Perhaps you're aware of sensations of warmth or coolness, feelings of lightness or heaviness, or even the pulsation of circulation.*

. . . Just explore any sensations here. Or no sensations at all.

. . . Now, allow your attention to move away from your feet and guide it to your lower back.

. . . Being curious about any tightness . . . tension . . . warmth . . . coolness . . . movement . . . pressure . . . that might be here right now.

. . . Just letting yourself explore it with your attention. If you notice your mind has drifted, gently but firmly bring it back.

. . . Now, allow your attention to move away from your back and let it come to rest on your shoulders.

. . . Letting your attention come to rest on the right shoulder . . .

. . . Just being curious about any sensations here . . . tightness, heaviness, lightness, pulling, stretching, warmth, or coolness. Noticing if the sensations are strong or gentle, if they are moving or in one place.

. . . And now letting your attention explore the left shoulder.

. . . Just being curious about any sensations here: tightness, heaviness, lightness, pulling, stretching, warmth, or coolness. Noticing if the sensations are strong or gentle, if they are moving or in one place.

. . . Allowing your shoulders to relax as you rest your attention here,
on both shoulders.

. . . Now guiding your breath back to the belly, and letting your
attention rest once again on the movements of the in-breath and the
out-breath.

. . . Simply paying attention,
As best you can,
Until the sound of the bell.

Practice #2: Mindful Eating

You can also practice paying attention, with curiosity and nonjudgment, to eating. You can try this with a single item of food, like one raisin or one piece of fruit, or with a whole meal or snack. Just remember
that we're practicing *first-person* noticing of the food and any physical
sensations as we do this one thing: eating mindfully. You may also
notice thoughts or feelings that you become aware of during this practice. See if you can attend to the quality of each moment, as well. Is it
pleasant, unpleasant, or neutral?

Before you begin, take a moment to adjust your posture and check
in with the breath in the body, wherever it's most noticeable. Then,
with full attention to the movement, pick up the item and hold it in
your hand. Notice the weight, shape, color, texture, size, and smell,
taking as much time as you need to explore each of these qualities.

Then slowly raise the object and place it in your mouth. Just allow it to remain there for a moment, noticing any sensations in your mouth. Then, mindfully, bite down and begin to chew, at the same time being aware of all the sensations associated with this action. Be aware of its quality: pleasant, unpleasant, or neutral. When you swallow the food, notice any movement in your body. Allow yourself to feel any and all sensations associated with this mindful experience of eating.

Practice #3: Mindful Inquiry

Investigate how these questions (or variations of them) might spark student motivation and interest by using them in your classroom:

What am I (are you) noticing right now?

What interests you about the story, lesson, or presentation?

How do you know that you're interested or not? What is the quality of your attention? What are some thoughts, feelings and physical sensations associated with interest?

What was your experience during this lesson?

What is important to you about this work/topic/project?

What are you feeling in your body when you are interested in something?

How do thoughts (not liking or liking) get in the way of being interested?

What are some ways to increase interest? To decrease interest?

Tips to Take Away

Motivation is important to learning because it orients attention and selects certain features of the environment on which to focus. As children get older, intrinsic sources of motivation become more influential. Our innate capacity for interest supports motivated behavior and can be fostered through mindful practice. One of the most fundamental attitudes of mindfulness practice is the suspension of automatic judgment in the service of openhearted curiosity. The practice of curious investigation, applied to first person experience, can strengthen attention, creativity, and awe in the classroom.

Skillful Responding:
The Mindful Way of
Dealing with Challenges

Mindfulness, the awareness that is *right here and right now, nonjudgmental,* and *open,* sounds relaxed, calm, and actually pretty great. Many moments invite mindful savoring, such as when we begin our long-awaited vacation, when we enjoy a delicious meal, or when we score the winning points for our team. But what happens when we really don't want to be in *this particular moment*? For most teachers and students, it's an experience we know all too well. Let's imagine that *this* is the moment a parent challenges you in a meeting or the moment you learn that a colleague was diagnosed with a serious illness. For students, maybe *this* is the moment you make a mistake in class, do something awkward in front of your friends, or learn that you were left out of a social gathering. These examples illustrate

the range of human experience. Much of our daily experience is less emotionally charged, but for the sake of simplicity, let's work with the examples above.

A vacation, a good meal, and a win are very pleasant, so we might meet
these moments with anticipation and delight. We typically want to have
more experiences like these. Dealing with difficult people can make us
anxious, and we gear up for the possibility of a parent-meeting confrontation. Hearing bad news unnerves us, and we find all manner of reasons to
put off calling the sick colleague. The in-class mistake, the public display of
awkwardness, or the exclusion from a peer group can also upset students,
who may feel like running away and hiding.

Each moment comes with its own feeling quality—pleasant, unpleasant, or neutral—even if we're not always aware of it. The basic attitude we
humans share about experience is that we want more of the pleasant variety
and less (or none) of the unpleasant. In fact, "stress" could be just another
name for "unpleasant." It's important to note that there's no advantage in
seeking out unpleasant experiences and nothing wrong with enjoying, sus-
taining, and appreciating the pleasant ones. In fact, mindfully savoring positive experience promotes resilience (Smith & Bryant, 2016). But, when we
have problems coping without drama when the inevitable difficulties of life
arise, or when we voluntarily add to our own stress burden, some balance
needs to be restored.

Fueled by the expectation that we *can* make unpleasant things go away,
we often try very hard to manage our stress or unpleasant experience by
trying to fix it. After one round of a diet regimen, we regain most of the

weight, and move on to another diet, and then another, with the same results. We use alcohol and other substances to help us relax and fix our troubles by forgetting, only to wake up in the middle of the night with the problems racing around in our heads. We become chronically irritable and overcontrolling toward a student who has a knack for getting on our nerves, anticipating her every annoying move in advance. There's a cyclical quality to our stress management, characterized by repeated efforts to transform unpleasant situations into those that suit us better. Sometimes we manage to make this strategy work, but in the long term we usually end up facing the same problems over and over again, frustrating ourselves in the process.

It is sensible and intelligent to apply the skills of fixing and problem solving to those things that are amenable to change. Certainly, there's no advantage in mindless acceptance of that which is inefficient or harmful to oneself or others. This is why we teach students to plan, reason, and problem solve (Elias & Tobias, 1996; Kendall & Braswell, 1982). For the most part, such approaches rely on logical thinking and are most successfully applied to well-defined problems with well-defined solutions, such as how to study, solve math problems, and eat healthfully. But not all teacher or student problems are *well-defined* (Kitchener, 1983). Some of the very real challenges of life and the classroom are *ill-defined* problems that have emotional underpinnings and no clear-cut answers. How can I handle my angry students? How can I manage to sustain empathy for parents who are uninvolved? How can I maintain my sense of balance when I'm constantly being asked to do more? Mindfulness offers another way to approach the difficult, ill-defined problems and uncomfortable feelings of real life, both

MOVING FROM THEORY TO PRACTICE
The Importance of Ethics

Any classroom program or practice that involves social and emotional skill development needs to rest on the ethical foundation that places the well-being of students first and foremost. Mindfulness is no exception. Mindfulness is not about controlling students' behavior, sharing personal information, identifying or solving individual students' psychological problems, introducing exotic or quasi-spiritual ideas, or creating a role for the teacher as guru. All these represent misinformed and potentially harmful notions that have no place in schools. The goal of schooling, historically, has been to prepare children for their future roles as productive members of society. We now benefit from information that clearly shows how emotions connect to learning and future productivity, and we have new ways to address this reality.

Perhaps we can compare SEL and mindfulness skills to public health initiatives like hand-washing. Hand-washing is a preventive measure found to reduce incidence of infectious disease. It is something that makes sense for everyone to do because of the way infections work. There is low risk of side effects and much to be gained from this practice. SEL and mindfulness are preventive measures that promote well-being, learning, and healthy functioning; like hand-washing, they can reduce the incidence and severity of later problems. It makes sense to teach these skills because of the ways our brain-based social, emotional, and learning processes work. Because the field of SEL is new, however, researchers continue to explore the best ways to reduce any potential risk associated with these approaches. Because of the general nature of mindfulness programs in classrooms, we need to be concerned about doing good and avoiding harm, given the diverse histories of our students. It's important to consider school context and to present a well-informed and well-pitched rationale for this work, devoid of jargon but clearly transparent in its objectives. We also should provide the option for adolescents not to practice mindfulness should they not wish to do so, so long as they don't prevent others from trying.

---

for teachers and students. It begins by recognizing that uncomfortable feelings may be a signal that you need to act in some way, but *that feelings are not, in themselves, the problem*.

Many of the risky and potentially dangerous behaviors of adolescents—procrastination, disruptiveness, disordered eating, cutting, drinking, violence, taking drugs, technological addiction, and so on—have a common denominator. They likely involve avoiding unpleasant emotional experience by trying to make it go away. The extent to which we do this is a measure of our *distress tolerance* (García-Oliva & Piqueras, 2016; Simons & Gaher, 2005). We all have our limits, but individuals who are highly intolerant of distress and unable to cope adaptively have quick triggers and are more likely to suffer from a range of psychological and behavioral problems (Zvolensky & Hogan, 2013). We know that we are primed to react consciously and unconsciously to threat. High levels of stress or trauma can sensitize people to stress, making the slings and arrows of life more difficult for them to bear. Sometimes, risky behavior like drug abuse can start as an attempt to silence the memories of past pain. But our generally allergic reaction to unpleasantness can also be manifested in more ordinary ways, like avoiding boring homework, cutting classes, or misbehaving. Student behaviors that attempt to make unwanted, uncomfortable feelings like inadequacy, boredom, restlessness, or anxiety go away are common, and they are also supported by certain implicit assumptions. Specifically, we appear to endorse the culturally reinforced belief that unpleasant things *should* go away. When we can't make the unpleasant parts of life go away, we often pile on some judgment, criticizing ourselves and others for life's imperfect circumstances.

It bears repeating that it's not harmful to try to fix problems or make things better. This is just common sense. The problem is that without some awareness of our knee-jerk inclination to perceive unpleasant things as threatening, our attempts to fix certain things can make them worse. Imagine this hypothetical scenario. A student is walking up the school stairway surrounded by classmates. He stumbles badly, falls and hits his knee, dropping the athletic equipment and books he is carrying, and lands face downward on the stairs. The rest of the kids turn to see what happened. Some ask if he's okay; others start to giggle and poke fun at him. His face feels flushed, his heart races, and his knee really hurts. He hurriedly pulls himself together and moves along as quickly as he can. From the outside, it looks like he's recovered. But on the inside, his mind races: *They must think I'm really stupid. Come on, don't be a baby. Suck it up and get back up. Don't show them you got hurt. I know someone tripped me. I'll show them.*

The mental chatter resumes later as he thinks about his friends' teasing, fueling his internal distress. Every time he passes that stairway, he remembers himself sprawled on the stairs. He's sure everyone else remembers it, too. Ruminative processing about how he could be so clumsy plays out in an endless mental loop. He attempts to avoid and suppress the embarrassment of the incident by placing the blame on others and plotting some revenge. Not only is the fall unpleasant in terms of the physical sensations in the body, but his discomfort is amplified by his evaluative stream of thoughts. Mental elaboration sustains the unpleasantness of the physical injury, creating emotional distress. Pain is felt in the knee, but suffering is in the mind. It's a double whammy. His automatic thoughts and emotions trigger the physiological cascade associated with the stress response. His mind continues its playback loop in an effort to justify his experience and avoid feelings of shame and helplessness. And, perhaps most importantly, these efforts are largely ineffective, because the painful memory surfaces again and again. Students are not the only ones who handle perceived threats by trying to avoid uncomfortable feelings. Similar thought streams (e.g., *I shouldn't have to put up with this. Things shouldn't be so hard*) might also sound familiar to teachers.

You might be wondering what the alternative is, given our ingrained human habit of trying to change or avoid the unpleasant. Maybe it's not too surprising that contemporary researchers have recognized what many traditional approaches to well-being have long stated: avoidance of negative or uncomfortable emotions is usually not helpful, let alone possible (Hayes, 1994). While avoidance of unpleasant thoughts, feelings, and sensations may produce some immediate gratification, chronic avoidance is associated with a number of problematic outcomes when it becomes a coping style (Spinhoven, Drost, de Rooij, van Hemert, & Penninx, 2014). This knowledge might be particularly important for adolescents, whose brains are especially sensitive to emotional experience and whose habits of coping are becoming established.

Adolescents report more daily experience of negative affect from ages 10 to 18 (Larson, Moneta, Richards & Wilson, 2002) but have more difficulty identifying and sorting out their feelings of anger, sadness, fear, disgust, and upset compared to younger children and adults (Nook, Sasse, Lambert, McLaughlin & Somerville, 2018). Presumably, the adolescent experience of negative affect involves co-occurring emotions that are more complex than those experienced in childhood and that pose greater coping challenges. As described in the hypothetical example, commonly used adolescent strategies for coping with distress (e.g., emotion avoidance, emotion suppression, and rumination) are maladaptive and related to more problems down the line. Although avoidance of emotional experience may offer short-term relief, the longer term consequences can include depression, anxiety, restricted opportunity, and poor social relationships (Eastabrook, Flynn, & Hollenstein, 2014). Rumination, or the repetitive focus on negative events, thoughts, or feelings in order to reduce the pain of a situation, is a well-known risk factor for depression and anxiety among youth and adults (Rood, Roelofs, Bögels, Nolen-Hoeksema, & Schouten, 2009). A recent examination of multiple studies showed that the maladaptive strategies many youth employ to manage their emotional distress actually play a *causal role* in the development of subsequent problems (Shäfer, Naumann, Holmes, Tuschen-Caffier, & Samson, 2017). Many major mental disorders have their start in adolescence, and less severe symptoms of disorders like anxiety and depression are alarmingly common (Lee et al., 2014; Spear, 2009).

The mental advances that secondary school teachers recognize in their students, such as the ability to reason abstractly or to take the perspective of others, also come with a price. Because youth *can* think abstractly, they can also engage in hypothetical thinking (e.g., *What if I were richer or thinner, like her?*) and can reach counterfactual conclusions (e.g., *Then I would be happier*). The very same mentalizing skills that allow students to take the perspective of Atticus Finch in Harper Lee's novel, *To Kill a Mockingbird,* allow them to imagine and mull over what their peers and teachers are thinking *about them* (Blakemore & Mills, 2014). Social media offers a ready platform for comparing oneself to others, a process called *social comparison.* Social comparison processes, already elevated during adolescence, are exacerbated by excessive media use and linked to depressive symptoms (Nesi & Prinstein, 2015). Cyberbullying is perceived as especially threatening to adolescents because one's shaming is on public display, comparison with others is exposed, and social isolation is threatened (Nilan, Burgess, Hobbs, Threadgold, & Alexander, 2015).

Overall, despite many obvious advantages, adolescent changes in cognitive and emotional development can lead to increased rumination and emotional distress for some youth. Just as educators work diligently to prepare students with academic knowledge and skills for the next stage of their life, so, too, should we prepare them with other life skills related to healthy emotion regulation. The importance of this social and emotional skill set can't be overestimated for adolescents, who are at an age when emotionality increases and adult patterns of emotion regulation are beginning to be consolidated (Paus, Keshavan, & Giedd, 2008).

How Mindfulness Helps Regulate Emotions

A major developmental advance during adolescence is the increasing ability to reason, make decisions, and think abstractly. These kinds of cognitive processes are rational and logical, referred to as "cool cognitions" (e.g., *These are the factors that led to the civil war,* or, *Here are some steps I can take to break down this project*), and they are often taught in decision making and study skills courses (Bergman & Rudman, 1985). When thinking and decision making are done in an emotional context, as in a group of peers, cognition can be less rational. The so-called emotional or "hot cognitions" can distort thinking and underlie many impulsive acts (e.g., *Forget about that homework. Let's party!*). It's difficult for most of us, but especially for adolescents, to override powerful emotions in order to think coolly and rationally, even if we know better. The student who keeps checking her phone in class can't seem to resist seeing her best friend's messages despite her teacher's disapproval. The student who fell on the stairs may not easily let go of his angry thoughts. In an effort to feel more of the pleasant things, like excitement, and fewer of the unpleasant things, like rejection or shame, adolescents may behave in ways that prove unproductive, especially if these behaviors ultimately become well-established patterns.

IT'S YOUR CHOICE

Some students burst into Vivian's 9th grade algebra class clearly upset about something. She wonders if it has anything to do with the noise she'd heard coming from the hallway. Vivian feels pressured to begin the lesson because the class period is short today. There was an assembly in the morning that cut into her teaching time.

Okay, everyone, let's calm down, Vivian says authoritatively, *we need to get started. Please take out your homework.*

But this group of students is having none of it. They seem to be oblivious, still in the throes of an animated discussion. Finally, she realizes that she's not going to get very far unless she asks them what has happened. Students describe an incident of teasing that got out of hand at lunch and that many other students in her class witnessed. A group of 10th grade students began calling the younger ones derogatory names, grabbing lunches and backpacks and throwing them into the trash. Some fighting, yelling, and retaliation ensued, alerting the teacher on duty who had been temporarily out of the room. The staff, unable to get a straight answer about what really happened in the altercation, issued detentions to everyone involved. Vivian's students are upset about the perceived unfairness and are finding it hard to settle down.

Although she wants the commotion to end, she also sees an opportunity. She agrees to listen to more of their story, but first suggests they all take a few relaxing sighs to calm down. Then she includes some guidance as they sit quietly:

Unfairness can makes us feel angry and may make us want to retaliate. At this moment, let's just notice any angry feelings that might be present in the body right now. Check in with yourself to sense any tension, tightness, heat, or movement. Where is it in your body? Perhaps you notice that you're breathing very fast . . . Or maybe that your heart is racing. Without trying to get rid of any feelings, just let yourself feel what's there.

After a few moments, she asks them again to take a few more relaxing sighs.

Vivian says: *When we experience difficulties like this, we do have a choice. We can react or respond.*

She asks students their ideas about the difference.

Someone volunteers: *I guess reacting means really getting all worked up about something.*

Yeah, adds a student, *like when we hit the kids who took our stuff and then we all got in trouble.*

Vivian continues: *Sometimes that just stresses us out more. When we practiced a little mindfulness right now, we were helping ourselves respond instead of react on automatic pilot. Maybe there's a way we can do something to help the adults understand how we feel. How could we respond mindfully without hurting ourselves or anyone else?*

Mindfulness gets to the root of these tendencies by encouraging exploration and acceptance of all feelings, without judgment. Mindful awareness of one's thoughts and emotions includes not just being present and curious about pleasant experience, but about *all* experience. This is a hard but crucial truth. Mindfulness is not about feeling a certain way; it's about feeling whatever is present in your life right now in order to have greater discernment about how to respond. This involves changing our relationship to feelings, perhaps especially to unpleasant ones. Rather than trying to escape as soon as we notice them, we actually acknowledge them, and perhaps even make some peace with them. This is what the practice of awareness and nonreactivity fosters.

Some studies show that simply being focused on observing thoughts, feelings, and physical sensations is not helpful and may even add to anxiety (e.g., *Oh no, here comes that anxious thought again!*). Importantly, it's *how we observe*—nonjudgmentally, with curiosity, and without reactivity—that promotes emotion regulation (e.g., *Where is the anxiety in my body right now? Can I be curious about it? Can I simply watch the anxious thoughts come and go?*) (Baer et al., 2008; Desrosiers, Curtiss, Vine, & Klemanski, 2014).

The process of observing emotions and thoughts nonreactively offers us a glimpse into the operations of our mind. Instead of being caught up as the lead performer in our mental drama, we have a front-row seat for the play. This permits greater perspective and deeper understanding. It also tempers the fear we often have of feeling our own feelings, because there is less automatic avoidance. If we *are* avoiding something, we notice that as well, but without commentary and without judging. Emotions become more tolerable because we have the courage to feel them, and from our new vantage point, we can see that they ebb and flow. There is less pressure to fix them and greater acceptance of our basic human experience.

Dispassionate observation and acknowledgement of experience, both pleasant and unpleasant, is a lot easier to do when the focus is on the breath or on some activity like eating. This is why teachers often start there. But the rubber really hits the road with stress. Compassionate acknowledgment of our unpleasant feelings and our typical ways of coping with them (e.g., harsh self criticism, lashing out, mental brooding, gossip, bullying, self-harm) is the doorway to reducing our reactivity and lessening our stress overall. We notice the inner mental and emotional experience, and, as best we can, we let it be. This practice has an interesting effect: It releases us from trying to solve the problem of unpleasant emotions. We struggle and stress less. We find less reactive and more regulated ways of working with difficult, ill-defined problems. We pull the plug, metaphorically speaking, to deactivate the stress cascade.

A Mindful Approach to Challenges

We know, at some deep level, that feeling our fear, anger, shame, irritation, anxiety, and sadness is better than masking it. But because it's not what we usually do, we need to practice. You can try a mindfulness experiment when you next experience something unpleasant (i.e., stress). Maybe your child is cranky before school and you have to rush to get yourself to work. *Unpleasant.* Perhaps a person who was supposed to help you with a project doesn't show up. *Unpleasant.* Perhaps your back pain returns or a student disrupts your class and you can't finish your lesson. *Unpleasant.* We can't escape all stress, but we don't need to make it worse. Remember that no one is advocating we deliberately try to make ourselves uncomfortable or search out unpleasant experiences in order to suffer more. There are plenty of naturally occurring events throughout the day when we don't get our own way. Simply acknowledging the affective quality of our experience (i.e., pleasant, unpleasant, or neutral) and the accompanying bodily sensations, thoughts, and feelings adds a different perspective to the experience, building resilience and grit (Duckworth, 2016). This kind of emotional resilience can protect adolescents from being overwhelmed by intense feelings of anger, sadness, or other distressing emotions that can lead to destructive actions.

LOSING IT . . . BUT NOT LOST

James spent a lot of time preparing materials for an experiment he learned at a professional development seminar. He enjoyed the demonstration so much that he was sure his students would like it, too. The materials were expensive, but he reasoned that the project could become a regular part of his curriculum.

When he introduces the experiment to his class, things go pretty well, although he notices that one of his more challenging students is distracted and is distracting others at his table. James reminds this student to pay attention several times, but to no avail. Clearly upset that this student is interrupting his long-planned demonstration, James walks over to his table as the rest of the class continues working. The inattentive student reminds James that he's missed two previous classes and isn't sure what he is supposed to do.

He's blaming me for not explaining the project clearly enough, James thinks. Using a harsh tone of voice, James tells the student that it's his fault for missing class and then turns and walks away. Embarrassed in front of his friends, the student angrily tosses his worksheet on the floor and, in the process, knocks over a piece of the new equipment. It crashes and breaks on the floor. The student looks sheepish and starts to apologize, but James is irate. His face gets flushed and his thoughts fill with anger: *This class is ruined . . . I worked so hard at it . . . He's so ungrateful and doesn't deserve to be here . . .* James sends the student out of the room.

After the bell rings and the students leave, James remembers the mindful awareness he has been trying to practice. He sits with his breath for a moment, letting himself feel his anger at the student's defiance and at himself for losing it. He practices what he learned about feeling the unpleasant without trying to block it out. He doesn't feel completely calm, but he's cooling down a bit. He begins to see that he reacted so strongly because he really wanted to do something interesting for his class. His intentions were good, but his thoughts about the whole class being a failure and his student being ungrateful might not really be true. This mindful pause allows him to see his reactivity with greater understanding and acceptance, and he decides to talk to the student about the problem.

Teachers are natural caregivers whose instincts are often oriented to making things better, so mindfulness of one's own tendency to avoid discomfort is also a good starting point. When it comes to emotions, not everything can be fixed or made pleasant, and we can't use performance-based thinking for emotional issues. Many adolescents have come to believe that only pleasant emotions are acceptable and that uncomfortable emotions are a sign of personal weakness or substandard performance in life. This fallacy presents a great but avoidable mental burden. It is critically important that students learn to recognize their uncomfortable feelings *in the moment* and understand that they do not have to *like* these feelings if they are to regulate distress in a balanced and wholesome way.

Teachers can help students understand their own tendency to cover up unpleasant feelings by modeling emotional balance. For example, teachers might respond to student pressure or complaints about schoolwork by acknowledging the obvious dissatisfaction without fixing or confrontation. It may be possible, when there is clearly something causing stress in the classroom, to recognize it openly, nonjudgmentally, and in the moment, thus modeling for students a mindful approach to unpleasant circumstances. The practices included in this chapter can provide the foundation for this emotional skill.

Sometimes pressures related to time or performance demands, fatigue, restlessness, and boredom build up in the classroom, and students react in negative ways. Simply avoiding the obviousness of the circumstances by pressing ahead can make matters worse. Allowing students to take a few mindful breaths or engage in some movement can demonstrate acceptance of the situation (e.g., *I know we've been working hard, and you're feeling tired*) and provide tools for stress management. Simple recognition of the body and feeling its sensations (e.g., *noticing feet on the floor, tension in the shoulders*) without changing anything can be a particularly effective antidote to stress. Body awareness or *interoception* helps students regulate their stress because it grounds attention in the physical body and reduces the amplification of distress caused by spiraling thought streams and emotional reactivity (Roeser & Pinela, 2014).

While classroom "peace corners" or places where students can go to self-regulate are becoming more popular for younger children (Lantieri, 2002), they are not usually available to adolescents. The purpose of a classroom peace corner is to provide students a safe place where they have an opportunity to handle strong emotions by recognizing them, accepting them, and restoring balance. They can then find a responsible way to act without hurting themselves or others. The opportunity to take a voluntary break to restore emotional control is certainly something adolescents need. Offering some nondisciplinary means for this process in secondary education settings could help adolescents develop better self-regulation and ultimately improve learning.

Reflecting on This Chapter

Try journaling your responses to the following questions:

Write a short description of a stressful classroom experience. What are some thoughts, feelings and physical sensations you notice when stress is triggered in the classroom? Use an example from your personal life if you wish.

How strong is my tendency to fix things just because they are unpleasant?

What might change in my work if I could be more present and less reactive to the unpleasant parts of my life?

What might change for my students it they could be more present and less reactive to the unpleasant parts of their lives?

**Questions available for download and printing at
http://wwnorton.com/rd/broderick**

Begin to Practice

Practice #1: Surfing the Waves of the Difficult

This is a formal practice that teachers can use to help with their own emotion regulation. Use a memory of something unpleasant to help you. Don't try to start with something big. You can use a memory of something mildly unpleasant.

Find your breath in the body wherever it's most noticeable.

Simply let your attention rest on the breath, allowing it to follow the in-breath and the out-breath for several breaths.

Feeling the movements of the breath in the body. Noting the quality of each breath. Shallow, deep, slow, fast, even, or choppy.

Whatever the breath is like, just noting it without changing anything.

We'll be using a memory of something stressful or unpleasant. Remembering that feelings are just like energy surges in the body. They come and go. At any time, you can return your attention to your breath.

Now allow yourself to remember an event in your life that was mildly stressful or unpleasant.

Notice if you can any feelings that arise in your mind and body as you remember this. Perhaps worry, sadness, fear, anger, or frustration.

Notice any sensations in your body that might be present as you remember this event. Heat or coolness, tightness, burning, or tension? Are they moving around or in one place?

Where are the sensations of unpleasantness in your body? Just be curious about them.

Can you simply explore the feeling without needing to change anything?

See if you can observe the feelings without covering them up.

Now return to the breath for a few cycles.

Practice #2: Dealing with the Difficult On the Spot (SOAR)

In daily life, the unpleasant—stress—happens, and you need to respond *on the spot*. Using the acronym SOAR, try the following steps.

> **S: See** what's happening for what it is: *unpleasant*.
>
> **O: Open** to the experience, and notice the feelings, thoughts, and body sensations arising in the moment.
>
> **A: Accept** the reality that *this is unpleasant*. You don't need to change how you feel. It's just the way you feel. Use your breath to help you stay balanced as you do this.
>
> **R: Respond** to the situation from this mindful perspective.

Practice #3: Befriending Pleasant and Unpleasant

This practice might best be done at the end of your day. Mentally scan the events of the day: morning, afternoon, and evening. Take a moment to recall the ones that were most *pleasant*. Savor each instance. Notice any sensations in your body, feel the feelings, and note any thoughts associated with these pleasant experiences.

Now take a moment to recall what was *unpleasant*. If you turned away from feeling the unpleasant feelings during the day, can you open to them now? Can you notice sensations in your body? Can you explore these sensations? Can you mentally hear the thoughts that accompany the uncomfortable experience? Can you explore these sensations and surf the waves of this experience? As you pay mindful attention, inwardly say, "I can surf the waves of my experience without hurting myself or others. I can let these thoughts and feelings come and go."

Now turn your attention to whatever happened during your day for which you are *grateful*. Savor each of these moments. Just rest for a few moments in the awareness of this gratitude as you conclude this practice.

Tips to Take Away

The willingness to be present to all experience, both pleasant and unpleasant, is a key characteristic of mindfulness. Avoidance of unpleasant experiences as a coping style has been linked to a number of emotional problems among youth as well as adults. Avoidance reduces tolerance for discomfort, amplifies internal distress, and compromises resilience. Acceptance of difficult emotions opens up more degrees of freedom for responding in a thoughtful and balanced way. Mindfulness of emotions strengthens awareness and acceptance of the whole range of human experience and is a key emotion regulation strategy for youth at a time of heightened emotionality and consolidation of adult coping patterns.

Connecting with Myself
and My Students

Approximately one hundred to two hundred students walk into each secondary school classroom over the course of a school day, according to national estimates of class size (National Center for Education Statistics, 2012). Each student is unique. In addition to observable differences like gender, race or ethnicity, and age, each has particular motivations, beliefs, and capabilities by virtue of having lived in different families and having had different experiences. We adults expect them all to learn, and teachers are charged with this task. This is a not a new problem for educators, and, overall, teachers have done remarkably well within the systems they have. Most students move on to lead productive lives that contribute to society. But as times change, so do the challenges those times introduce.

In the contemporary culture of assessment, students are measured on outcomes that define success in certain ways (Ravitch, 2010; Sawchuk,

2014). Critics have argued that prioritizing academic assessment can edge out other sources of creative expression, social support, and opportunities that existed for adolescents who grew up in different times (Noddings, 2015; Siegel & Scovill, 2000). The metrics we use to measure success at the secondary level, like test scores, GPAs, and college acceptance rates, are not able to capture some of our real intentions for youth. If you examine vision statements from school districts across the country, you'll inevitably find goals like: self-directed and lifelong learning, social responsibility, ethical behavior, care for the community, and whole child development.

Such aspirations are deeply resonant with the goals of social-emotional learning (SEL): self-management, relationship skills, responsible decision making, self- and social awareness (Collaborative for Academic, Social, and Emotional Learning, 2018) Given the profusion of demands at the secondary level, however, time and energy to focus on this fundamental skill set can come up short. Often, SEL skills are thought to be a better fit with curricula for younger children. Adolescents, one can argue, are much closer to that time of life when they will take on adult responsibilities. Therefore, we might assume that they already possess SEL skills or are more in need of the "hard" skills that prepare them for jobs or postsecondary education.

These entrenched assumptions may be shifting, as there is a growing recognition that secondary students also need grounding and practice in inter- and intrapersonal skills for life and for work (National Commission on Social, Emotional, and Academic Development, 2018). Educators have long known that optimal outcomes occur when the developmental needs of students are integrated into education, a theory called stage-environment fit (see Eccles et al., 1993). Recently, researchers have invested more attention in adolescent development, in part because of new methods for studying the teenage brain, and these findings are gradually making inroads into education to reduce the mismatch between schools and adolescent social-emotional needs.

Basic Needs of Adolescents

What, then, might it mean to meet the needs of the *whole adolescent*? Despite each student's uniqueness, they all share a common core of human needs: autonomy, competence, and connection (Deci & Ryan, 1991). Obviously, basic needs are expressed in different ways in different people and across different times in the life span. In the early school years, young children's attempts at autonomy (e.g., helping with classroom chores) are encouraged, carefully scaffolded, and supervised by primary teachers who are alert to their safety. Young children's autonomy is supported because it is a foundation for *self-esteem*. Competence in young children is acquired through time-tested programs for teaching academic (e.g., reading and writing), motor (e.g., catching a ball, cutting with scissors), emotional (e.g., expressing feelings), and social (e.g., sharing and cooperative play) skills. Young children's competence is supported because it is a foundation for *self-efficacy*. Emotional connection is fostered through warm and nurturant interactions with elementary school teachers who also set age-appropriate expectations for classroom behavior. Young children's connection is supported because it is the foundation for *self-* and *emotion regulation* and *prosocial behavior*. The ways we meet basic needs look different in the second decade of life, but their foundational role in the continuing development of self-esteem, self-efficacy, self-regulation, and concern for others is the same.

Research suggests that the fit between adolescents and their schools gets poorer from middle school onward (Eccles et al., 1993). Needs for autonomy get stronger, and adult authority is challenged. Adolescents come to view their decisions as their own business, and less authority is ceded to adults over time, especially in personal areas like dating and friendship relationships (Smetana, Crean, & Campione-Barr, 2005). The risk-taking, excitement-seeking side of adolescents can be seen in power struggles with teachers. Many secondary teachers have encountered adolescents who demonstrate annoying, provocative, or noncompliant behavior intended for an audience of peers. Although this is not unusual, it's not helpful for learning in the classroom. Therefore, common-sense classroom management techniques are appropriate and necessary. The reported tendency of secondary-level teachers to become more controlling and to resort to authoritarian approaches may arise from their own decreasing self-efficacy, from diminished confidence in their ability to motivate students, and from inappropriate autonomy-seeking behavior from youth (Wolters & Daugherty, 2007). Recommendations to increase opportunity for choice in the curriculum and allow for student-led activities, discussion, and projects within an acceptable structure are good ways for secondary educators to support self-esteem and agency.

The adolescent need for competence can assert itself in testing limits and seeking recognition as a person who matters. When competence and respect can't be attained in prosocial ways, youth may seek more problematic means. In addition to traditional academic learning, opportunities for vocational education, service, arts, athletics, community-based projects, and more can offer a broader set of occasions for relevance and accomplishment that enhance self-efficacy.

Needs for connection reflect the basic human requirement for warmth, validation, and love. The need to connect exists throughout the life span, and most emotional problems are associated, in some way, with needs for love and recognition that have largely gone unmet. Adolescents find themselves faced with the challenge of seeking emotional connections beyond the bounds of family. We remember our own adolescence and can relate to youth's intense pull toward the peer group, what Taffel (2002) calls the "second family." Some might assume that adolescents' connection to peers is enough to satisfy their emotional needs, but they also need caring adults. Metaphorically, adolescents are all in the same emotional boat, not completely adrift but clearly in need of guidance from shore. One large study of school climate in over 300 U.S. high schools found that having high expectations for students alone was not the answer to increased student engagement and achievement. The relationship quality between students and teachers was also a critical ingredient. In schools with high expectations alone, the drop out rate was almost 35% higher than in schools with high expectations *and* high levels of teacher-student relationship quality (Jia, Konold, & Cornell, 2016).

Educational experts have written extensively about teacher-student relationship quality, but what do students think about this topic?

MOVING FROM THEORY TO PRACTICE
The Importance of Time

Any commitment worth making takes time. However, time may be among the scarcest commodities in secondary schools today. At this point, we still don't know how much time for mindfulness practice is optimal, because this probably depends upon the age and stage of youth themselves. However, some researchers are suggesting that schools provide for some initial orientation to mindfulness followed by daily practice periods if they are serious about giving mindfulness a chance (Johnson, Burke, Brinkman, & Wade, 2017). Students have virtually no control over their time during the school day, so simply adding on a requirement to practice at home may be perceived as yet another burden (Bailey et al., 2018).

The ways in which educational institutions organize their time reflect, wittingly or unwittingly, their fundamental intentions. The intention to be more mindful can collectively translate into some concrete shifts in priorities, such as scheduling time for mindfulness practice during the school day. This may be one way for secondary schools to address the needs of the *whole adolescent:* by taking a critical look at how students' time during this sensitive period of development is spent and how those hours might be used more creatively.

Researchers (Raufelder et al., 2016) asked German secondary students to respond to questions like, "What constitutes a good teacher? How does a good teacher motivate his or her students?" Three main themes emerged from the interviews. Students gave priority to relational characteristics over teaching expertise and teacher personal characteristics in their definition of a good teacher. In their view, "good" secondary teachers showed: (1) appreciation for students, (2) consideration of student needs, and (3) warmth. Teachers who valued student effort and who offered encouragement were perceived as empowering. Students felt more efficacious and competent in their classrooms. Teachers who were aware of individual student needs, especially emotional ones, and who responded with understanding also ranked high on the scale of good teaching. The authors conclude that "overall, most students needed to feel that teachers were not only concerned with the learning material, but with their personal needs and problems" (p. 34).

Adolescents need caring and responsible adults to model self-regulation, to guide their passage, and to help them avoid dangerous waters. For some students, a teacher might be the only mentor available, possibly the last important relationship with an adult before they themselves enter adulthood (Roeser & Eccles, 2015). However, with so many students and so much to do, it is no surprise that secondary teachers can feel burdened by an additional responsibility for relationship. Teaching can be emotionally draining as it is, and adolescents can challenge authority in ways that make teachers feel inadequate. Ample research shows that high levels of stress and diminishing emotional resources can lead to burnout, which is highest in teachers compared to those in other professions (Aloe, Amo, & Shanahan, 2014). Burnout is reflected in feelings of exhaustion (e.g., not being able to offer any more of yourself) and lack of satisfaction (Maslach, Jackson, & Leiter, 1996). But perhaps the most pernicious aspect of teacher burnout, and the one that affects adolescents most deeply, has been called cynicism. This involves depersonalizing students and detaching oneself from them, as a means of self-protection. Over time, work overload, chronic stress, decreased sense of efficacy, and failure to meet performance goals can blunt our connections to our students and ourselves (Anderman & Maehr, 1994; Anderman & Midgley, 1997; Wigfield, Eccles, & Rodriquez, 1998; Wolters & Daugherty, 2007).

The level of stress experienced by teachers is also related to stress in students, as measured by stress hormones. Teachers who showed elevations on two facets of burnout, depersonalization and exhaustion, had stress-related cortisol patterns that were predictive of similarly elevated levels in their 4th to 7th grade students (Oberle & Schonert-Reichl, 2016). These findings suggest serious repercussions for teachers' own health and well-being as well as that of their students. When secondary teachers are exhausted and emotionally indifferent to students at a time when they need adult connection, youth stand to lose a lot.

One important and very basic contribution to connection that secondary teachers can offer is their own genuine understanding of the significance of the adolescent period, with all its risks and opportunities (Steinberg, 2014). The ability to look beyond the surface of adolescent behavior, to resist the temptation to view adolescents as slightly larger children or smaller adults, is an expression of compassion. This point of view considers normal developmental changes and the impact that life circumstances have had on the youth sitting before us. Quite often, adults view all young people as being carefree, without a worry in the world. But we would be remiss if we were to overlook the fact that many secondary students come to school having suffered trauma, victimization, abuse, discrimination, poverty, and neglect. Even materially advantaged students may have experienced the neglect of inconsistent limits or insufficient emotional support.

Wounds and other medical conditions cause certain parts of the body to become sensitive to pain, especially tender to the touch. We don't intentionally treat physical wounds roughly or abrade them in the hopes of making them better. Similarly, inner wounds can't be healed with rough treatment. This principle is especially true for those who have suffered trauma. Studies indicate that 70% of students with emotional, cognitive, or behavioral problems have had early adverse experiences in childhood (Bethell, Gombojav, Solloway, & Wissow, 2016). We should also bear in mind that these numbers reflect reported trauma. Much trauma goes unrecognized, so even this high statistic may underestimate of the scope of the problem.

Often, the misbehavior we see in some, but not all, students is like a giant stress response, resulting from these inner wounds and inadequate self-regulatory skills. Our own reactivity can also result from similar sensitizing. Clearly, the classroom teacher is not a therapist and can't solve all student problems, desperate though they might be. Many teachers may not see the promotion of social and emotional skills as part of their job. However, as has been repeatedly stated and confirmed by research, academic learning and emotional functioning are deeply interconnected. If we want students to succeed, we need to consider this brain-based reality. At the most basic level, this implies seeing each student as valuable and worthy of respect. As Noddings points out in a very mindful way: "I do not need to establish a deep, lasting, time-consuming personal relationship with every student. What I must do is to be totally and nonselectively present to the student—to each student—as he addresses me. The time interval may be brief, but the encounter is total" (Noddings, 1984, p.180).

COMPASSION HEALS

A few months ago, a new student joined Margaret's class. He had been a student at her school before but had spent the first two-thirds of this school year in a juvenile placement facility. Margaret tries to connect with him, even though he has had trouble with other teachers.

One day, the class is reviewing concepts by playing a Jeopardy game. Students are split into teams, except for the new student who tells Margaret he doesn't want to play. Margaret suggests that he just slide his chair over and join the group sitting near him. He says, again, that he doesn't want to play. He's defiant.

Margaret notices herself getting worked up and thinks, *Join a group or go to the office*. It seems to her to be the natural reaction to a student who refuses to do what he's been told. She recognizes that she doesn't want to react like that, given the rapport she'd built with him. Connecting with students and supporting their well-being is one of Margaret's strong intentions. So, she kindly asks him one more time to join the group.

He rolls his eyes and slides his chair over a few millimeters toward them. Margaret notices that he doesn't talk to the other students, but she doesn't force anything.

After class, Margaret checks his schedule, noting that he has study hall in the cafeteria. She asks him to step into the hallway and asks, *What's going on? Are you okay?*

He says he's just having a really bad day.

She asks if he has talked to anybody about it and he says no, that he doesn't really talk to anybody. She can see that he's fighting back tears. Margaret tells him that, even though she's only known him for a short period of time, she is willing to listen if he wants to talk. Margaret also says she cares about him and wants him to finish strong this school year.

The student thanks her for coming down to speak with him. Despite the fact that he hasn't shared more information with Margaret, he keeps coming to her class and is cooperative and respectful.

(Personal communication, N. Schuit)

Practicing Kindness and Compassion

Kindness and compassion can be deliberately cultivated to strengthen reserves for ourselves and our students. Mindfulness is inherently compassionate because nothing is excluded from awareness and nothing is rejected out of hand. In addition, specific contemplative practices can amplify compassion toward others and toward ourselves, especially under difficult circumstances. The root of the word compassion means "to suffer with," which implies a recognition that people are suffering and includes the wish to reduce their suffering (Goetz, Keltner, & Simon-Thomas, 2010; Neff, 2009).

Research has demonstrated that compassion is distinct from empathy, involves different neural circuitry, and produces different emotional outcomes (Weng et al, 2013). Empathy is the ability to resonate with another's emotional state, like the joy or sadness of a partner or even a stranger. The neural networks involved in the subjective experience of pain are activated when we witness the pain of others, whether the person is present or viewed in video or images (Lamm, Decety, & Singer, 2011). We literally share the affective and somatic experience through this empathic connection (de Vignemont & Singer, 2006). Empathy supports connection, but the powerful capacity for empathic resonance can lead to emotional exhaustion, low positive affectivity, and burnout when the observed pain is overwhelming. In resonating strongly with the pain of another, observers can experience greater negative affect as well as the desire to avoid the painful situation (Klimecki & Singer, 2012). Teachers can be at high risk of burnout because of their ability to empathize.

Compassion, in contrast, activates different neural networks and is associated with strong positive emotions as well as more regulated negative ones (Weng, Schuyler & Davidson, 2017). A study by Klimecki and colleagues (Klimecki, Leiberg, Ricard, & Singer, 2014) illustrates this effect. Adult participants received either affect or memory training in two phases over the course of the study. The affect group was first trained to be empathic, then trained in compassion. The memory group received two memory-related trainings and served as a control group. After each phase of training, participants were shown videos of distressing images while undergoing brain imaging . Empathy training, compared to memory training, resulted in higher levels of empathy but also higher levels of distress because certain parts of the brain related to the experience of pain were activated. Following empathy training, participants in the affect group were also more prone to experience empathic distress in daily life. The compassion training of phase two produced very different results for the affect group. Activation of different neural networks, associated with love and affiliation, increased positive emotions while modulating negative emotions. After practicing compassion, participants did not avoid the reality of the suffering, and the observed suffering did not overwhelm them.

Self-Compassion

For many people in the teaching profession, compassion for others is easier to access than compassion for themselves. This attitude may prove ultimately unhelpful, because disrespect for ourselves and disregard for our basic physical, social, and emotional needs underlies many self-destructive behaviors that take their toll on health and happiness. Self-compassion practice actively addresses the threats to emotional disconnection by operating as a protective factor, a sort of vaccine against the potentially debilitating circumstances that drain our resources. For adults, self-compassion practice has been associated with lower stress reactivity, reduced inflammation, and reductions in anxiety and mood disorders (Breines et al., 2015; Leaviss & Uttley, 2015; Pace et al., 2013). Research using neuroimaging techniques has also shown that such practice produces long-lasting alterations in brain function in areas related to development of positive affective states such as optimism, curiosity, interest, and excitement (Lutz et al, 2004). Self-compassion does not preclude people from experiencing uncomfortable feelings, but it helps regulate the experience. Perhaps teaching professionals need to be particularly mindful of their own needs for self-compassion because they so often share in the emotional experiences of others.

Self-compassion is distinct from self-esteem, which can sometimes depend on relative assessments of success or failure compared to others (Neff & Vonk, 2009). Downward social comparison (e.g., *At least I'm better than he is*) is a mental strategy we occasionally use to inflate our self-esteem at the expense of someone else (Aspinwall & Taylor, 1993). A healthy sense of self-esteem is certainly important but can be related to factors outside our control that ebb and flow, like material possessions and professional recognition. When we come up short and feel we are lacking in some important way, self-compassion can mitigate our tendency toward harsh self-criticism. We can meet our imperfections with acceptance and kindness instead of judgment, even as we aspire to improve. Self-compassion recognizes that each of us is worthy of kindness, even though we are all works in progress.

STUDENT SELF-CARE

Once a week, Paul's athletes spend some time before training talking about what mindfulness is and how it can help them. They also do some mindfulness practice. Paul is curious about what his students are learning and applying from the classes. He asks Ali about her experience one day after practice.

Ali responds: *I used to always think negatively, kind of. I wouldn't be very positive or happy. Something was always wrong. I would always think, since this bad thing is happening, this is going to happen all the time. I'm just terrible now.*

After doing mindfulness and practicing loving-kindness, I'm not making such a big deal of everything. If I made a bad play in a game, I used to make it last the whole entire game. I'd have my head down. I'd freak out. I'd be so upset.

But now, I breathe in, breathe out, 30 seconds, I give myself 30 seconds, and then I'm done, and then I can let it go. Not happy, but I'm new and starting over.

Throughout the day, I don't really let things get to me as much anymore. Like if people are rude or something, I'll breathe and stuff like that. I don't let it get to me so much any more.

Mindfulness helps me calm down and say to myself 'Okay, don't get mad.' Someone might just do something or say something, but it doesn't mean a lot. They're probably going to do it again. They're probably going to make me mad again. I just can't let them get to me.

I learned that I can treat my mind and my body with more respect.

(Adapted from a PA high school focus group)

Research has also shown promising benefits for self-compassion practice for adolescents themselves (Bluth, Gaylord, Campo, Mullarkey, & Hobbs, 2016; Galla, 2016; Reddy et al., 2013). This makes sense, given the thought streams of social comparison, self-criticism, isolation, and uncertainty that plague some youth. For adolescents, learning how to practice self-care is a good fit. First and foremost, self-care supports autonomy. In addition to learning other healthy ways of coping, the ability to offer oneself loving-kindness and compassion, as a regular practice and on the spot, can increase adolescents' sense of personal control. Recognizing that you have a way to handle your own stress or emotional upsets can be very empowering. As one high school student reflected after taking a mindfulness course, "I learned that I can control the way I react to things and that nothing is too overwhelming for me to handle." In self-compassion practice, no part of oneself is rejected or turned away. Bluth and colleagues (2016) point out that, in offering themselves loving-kindness and compassion, adolescents reconnect with themselves. Helping youth recognize that everyone, even the most popular student in class, has experienced failure, embarrassment, anxiety, and anger by virtue of their common humanity serves to reduce adolescent isolation. Thus, the intentional practice of kindness toward oneself builds tolerance and resilience in the face of difficulty.

Compassion for Our Students and Others

The internal experience of compassion for others should transfer into prosocial action because compassion, as Noddings (2015) points out, needs to move from *caring about* to *caring for*. Davidson has shown that people who engaged in mental compassion practice behaved in more prosocial ways compared to individuals who were taught an alternative mental practice. The groups who practiced compassion were more likely to offer to help an injured person, help others in games, and sustain charitable donations compared to control groups. Compassion training in young children resulted in more classroom sharing (Lavelle, Flook, & Ghahremani, 2017). Compassion practice may make us more attentive to others' emotional needs and more responsive to them.

Skeptics will be happy to know that one doesn't need to feel all warm and fuzzy in order to benefit from compassion practices. Compassion is a choice we make to act in a certain way: with kindness instead of criticism, with care instead of automatic judgment and blame, from the perspective of "we" in addition to "me." Showing kindness and compassion is not about letting oneself or students off the hook for harmful behavior or irresponsibility. As every authoritative parent knows, one of the best things you can provide for children is a set of well-defined limits. A venerable research tradition has demonstrated that both appropriate levels of demandingness (i.e., rules and limits) in concert with high levels of nurturance are the mark of optimal parenting, in childhood and in adolescence. So, although compassion practice softens the heart to be more aware of suffering, it doesn't mean being soft, and it's not about sentimentality. Compassionate awareness of ourselves and our students helps us make better informed decisions by opening our perspective to dimensions that we otherwise might not have seen.

Compassion and its expression can be affected by levels of closeness to the situation. We care a great deal about people close to us, so kindness and compassion may feel effortless. We are also able, with some ease, to feel compassionate at the intellectual level. Hearing about a troubled student's background, we recognize his or her hardship and comprehend, to the degree we can, its impact on the student's current behavior. Through nonjudgmental listening and acts of kindness, we may be able to practice compassion quite easily when students are in need and receptive to our efforts. But most of us have a harder time feeling and behaving in a compassionate way when students and others take out their own distress on us, or when we take their behavior personally. The chronically indifferent or surly student, the one who stops coming to class, and so on, can be perceived as making a statement about our teaching quality. All the techniques we've learned for classroom and behavior management can escape us if we lose perspective. We actually become less effective in these circumstances, because our thinking is clouded and our ability to access a way of responding that might actually improve the situation eludes us.

How can we be more compassionate both in good times and in times of provocation? A moment of self-compassion can make compassion for others easier. Take a self-compassion break (adapted from Neff, 2015), by recognizing your own suffering in the moment (e.g., *This feels hurtful*), remembering that you are not the only one who feels like this (e.g., *Others feel this, too*), and then offering kindness to yourself (e.g., *May I be kind to myself right now*). The reflection questions that follow offer opportunities to consider how the intentional practice of kindness can benefit your teaching and help you meet students' need for relationship. The formal loving-kindness practice can strengthen personal inner resources like life satisfaction and meaning (Fredrickson, Cohn, Coffey, Pek, & Finkel, 2008) and can be taught to students. In addition to kindness and compassion, the practice of gratitude and other healthy emotions can become part of the classroom routine, amplifying the student-teacher connection.

Reflecting on This Chapter

Try journaling your responses to the following questions:

What do I remember most about my experience as a student in high school (or middle school)? What would I have appreciated from my teachers at that time in my life?

As I allow myself to be more open to the possibility of practicing mindfulness and compassion more deliberately, what, if any, concerns do I notice about losing control of the classroom? About disliking some of my students? About my students disliking me? About getting too close to the students? These concerns may or may not arise, but it's useful to explore which assumptions might be an obstacle to connecting with students as a responsible and caring adult. Include, if you can, some thoughts about what might underlie these assumptions (e.g., expectations of yourself and others, confusing perception of roles, fear of vulnerability). After this exploration, see if you can bring some kindness and acceptance to these emotional states. Which student behaviors might signal the need for a stronger emotional connection with me? In which situations or with which particular student do you wish to practice kindness? What form will this take?

Questions available for download and printing at
http://wwnorton.com/rd/broderick

Begin to Practice

Practice #1: Loving-kindness

Loving-kindness may be defined as an attitude that extends care and compassion toward oneself and others (Goleman, 2003). In this loving-kindness practice, we offer kindness to ourselves first and then to others. We often cultivate unhelpful thoughts and feelings, like self-criticism and harsh judgment, when we fail to live up to our expectations. Without awareness, we continue to practice these unhelpful thoughts and feelings unconsciously. Loving-kindness practice offers an opportunity to practice kindness instead of meanness. Don't worry if you don't feel particularly kind or gentle toward yourself when you begin. Don't worry if you don't feel anything in particular in the beginning or even if you feel awkward doing this practice. Over time, the practice of compassion for yourself and others can help you be more balanced in your responding and enhance the concern you already have for others, especially students in your care. The patient qualities you cultivate in this practice can help you be more accepting of your humanity and reduce the burden of stress and suffering that self-criticism engenders.

So sit quietly, and tune into the breath.

Let your attention rest on in-breath and the out-breath as you take five deep, full breaths.
(Pause for five breaths)
We'll be bringing to mind something we've experienced before and letting that help us practice kindness right now.

Bring to mind a time when someone was kind to you.

It doesn't have to be something big. It could be a small act of kindness from a friend, a relative, a student (teacher), a colleague (coach) or even a stranger.

This memory you are recalling could be something that happened recently or even a long time ago.

Just do your best to remember the experience in as much detail as you can.

As you sit here with this memory,
Notice what you are sensing in your body right now,
Maybe some lightness,
Some warmth.

Notice thoughts that may be present in your mind,

Notice any emotions that may be present.

If you can't remember anything or if you can't locate it in your body, that's fine.
Just pay attention to your breath.
Whatever you are experiencing right now is fine.

So holding the memory of this experience in your mind, if you can,
Take this felt sense of kindness, of care, and offer it back to yourself.

Directing these wishes to yourself while inwardly repeating the phrases:

I wish to treat myself with kindness.

I wish to be peaceful.

I wish to be strong and balanced.

I wish to be happy and at ease.

Then, taking this felt sense of kindness and directing it to the person who was kind to you. (This could also be someone who needs your kindness, or even someone who has not been kind).

I wish that you, too, be treated with kindness.

I wish that you, too, be peaceful.

I wish that you, too, be strong and balanced.

I wish that you, too, be happy and at ease.

Now, once again, bringing your attention to the breath as you repeat the phrases for a few more cycles.

After practicing this yourself, you may wish to use it with students.

■   Adapt the phrases for students if you wish.

■   Invite students to compose and use their own wishes.

■   Provide students with slips of paper and invite them to write a general kindness wish that would be suitable for anyone in the class. Place the folded strips in a basket so that each student can take one as they leave the room.

Practice #2: Compassion for a Difficult Student

Teachers are advised, from their earliest days in the profession, not to take things personally. This is far easier said than done. Sometimes it seems that students are having fun at our expense and preventing us from doing our job. We generally feel angry or frightened when we feel challenged or disrespected. However, our reaction may not be commensurate with the adolescent offense, given their developmental level, and can distort our perception of the situation, contribute to anger or withdrawal, and reduce feelings of connection. Compassion practice can be a resource in these difficult situations.

This practice is intended to help ease the conflict you may feel with a student or someone who is causing you difficulty. This practice is not intended to make you immune to student misbehavior or to your responsibility to hold students accountable for their behavior. Rather it is intended to help you become aware of all the dimensions of the struggle, to offer some kindness to yourself and the other person, and then to help you take some action from a benevolent position. Benevolence is a more confident position for action than anger or withdrawal. Remember that both you and your student deserve care, concern, and respect.

The ABC's of On-The-Spot Compassion

A: *Awareness.* Bring awareness to the difficult emotions you are experiencing in the moment (e.g., feeling insulted, disrespected, powerless, frightened, inadequate).

B: *Breathing in, breathing out.* Inwardly link these wishes to the in-breath and the out-breath.

Breathing in, I offer myself kindness.

Breathing out, I offer you compassion.

You may continue this as long as you need to help yourself restore some balance. You can also shorten the phrases to " . . . *kindness . . . compassion"* or choose your own words. It may also be helpful to visualize the breath moving in an out as you offer kindness to yourself and your student.

C: *Connect.* When you feel more ready, respond to the student in the moment with as much authentic concern as possible and as much limit-setting as needed.

Practice #3: Daily Doses of Kindness: A New Kind of Suggestion Box

Most ideas for improvement in schools relate to academic performance, efficiency, or behavior management. You can adapt this idea to support the emotional and social skills students have been practicing. Keep a "suggestion box" with paper and pencil in the classroom and invite students to contribute their suggestions for ways the class can practice kindness, compassion, and gratitude. Teachers can select a suggestion on a regular basis for the group to discuss, implement, and practice.

Examples include:

- Taking on a project as a group that could benefit someone else (e.g., teaching younger students, organizing and coordinating a service project).

- Writing gratitude letters or sharing experiences of gratitude.

- Scheduling regular class times for conversations about what works and what isn't working in the classroom.

- Including students in the creation of projects and assignments to make them more meaningful.

- Brainstorming strategies for the students to use to help each other in authentic ways.

Tips to Take Away

Adolescents' basic needs for autonomy, competence, and connection are important to address as part of their educational experience. The need for connection, to be valued and respected, is an essential part of the teacher-student relationship. Adolescents need caring and connection from adults at a time when pressures for academic performance may take center stage. But the emotional cost of caring can be daunting for teachers. The deliberate practice of kindness and compassion can support mental and physical health for teachers and students and strengthen the emotional connections important during this point in development. Savoring the positive moments of life mindfully, expressing gratitude, cultivating optimism, and accepting the less pleasant realities of life are all tools that can build resilience (Fredrickson, 2003; 2013).

Claiming Leadership
Through Mindful Teaching

The years that students spend in formal schooling provide them with what Lortie (1975) calls an "apprenticeship of observation" that extends beyond simply observing teaching techniques. In watching teachers on a daily basis, adolescents learn a lot more than academic knowledge. They learn how we adults speak to one another; how we care for others; how we manage challenges and make decisions and, to some degree, even what we value. Teacher behaviors and attitudes related to self-awareness and management, decision making, social relationships, and responsibility are important life lessons for student apprentices. Even though we might not refer to these lessons as social-emotional learning, we know that students do remember, long after they leave school, what teachers have taught them about being adult. The movement toward teaching social-emotional skills along with academics may reflect the recognition that teachers routinely model social and emotional dispositions in their interactions with students. Therefore, it's time to make this particular kind of education more intentional. Mindfulness can infuse all the dimensions of SEL with more depth and, potentially, greater reach and sustainability (Greenberg, 2014; Lawlor, 2016). This chapter will provide some examples.

Mindful, contemplative practices complement conceptual ways of teaching because of the emphasis placed on *first-person experience*. Schooling perfects certain kinds of mental operations, notably the "doing" skills of remembering, conceptualizing, and analyzing, because these mental skills are important for academic success. SEL skills may also be taught from a conceptual point of view, through discussions of certain character traits, analyses of the disadvantages of taking drugs, or through memorization of the steps of a problem-solving model. Contemplative practices engage another mode of mind—one that is observant and curious about sensory events, thoughts, and feelings in real time and in a nonjudgmental way (Williams, 2010). The latter operating mode is the "being" mind, one that we often forget we have because of all our doing. The being mode of mind deepens learning by adding meaningful personal experience to conceptual awareness, allowing us to move from talking *about* experience to *experiencing*.

Even though mindful awareness helps us pay attention to the texture of personal, subjective experience in a particular way, it's clear from the previous chapters that mindfulness is not an exercise in self-absorption. Becoming more aware of, and more accepting of, our own subjective experience lessens the grip of rigid thinking, implicit biases, knee-jerk responses, and unhealthy patterns of cognition, affect, and behavior. This is good news for everyone. As we practice mindfulness in our life, we can become more wise and more human, in the best sense of these words.

Consider Jon Kabat-Zinn's expanded definition:

> Mindfulness is a way of being in wise and purposeful relationship with one's experience, both inwardly and outwardly. It is cultivated by systematically exercising one's capacity for paying attention, on purpose, in the present moment, and nonjudgmentally, and by learning to inhabit and make use of the clarity, discernment, ethical understanding, and awareness that arise from tapping into one's own deep and innate interior resources for learning, growing, healing, and transformation, available to us across the lifespan by virtue of being human. . . . Awareness in its purest form, or mindfulness, thus has the potential to add value and new degrees of freedom to living life fully and wisely and, thus, to making wiser and healthier, more compassionate and altruistic choices. . . . (Kabat-Zinn, 2015)

Moving beyond self-interest, even during the adolescent period of self-absorption, is possible and beneficial in helping young people respond to life's big questions (e.g., Where am I going in life?). Purpose provides meaning and motivation for outcomes that are relevant to oneself and, importantly, for consequences that ripple beyond oneself (Damon, Menon, & Cotton Bronk, 2003). A sense of purpose is associated with achievement, well-being, and hopefulness in youth as well as resilience in teachers (Burrow, O'Dell, & Hill, 2010; Tirri & Ubani, 2013). Consolidating a sense of purpose is a developmental goal for adolescents and young adults, and intentionality is a foundation for purposeful action. In considering their important role as models for youth, teachers can be well served by remembering, on a regular basis, their intentions for teaching.

To experiment with this kind of recollection, take a moment to write your responses to the following hypothetical question:

> *Imagine that you just received a new job description. It reads: You will no longer be responsible for teaching your particular academic subject area. Instead, your primary job description is to be a role model for adolescents who are looking to you for information about what it's like to be an adult. Identify three to five of your core values to serve as the basis of your "new" curriculum. If you get stuck, ask yourself the question as many times as needed, and write what arises in you.*

Your answers are the foundation for authentic intentions, which might be revisited on a regular basis to motivate you amidst the busyness of daily life. When developing classroom guidelines with students, at certain transition points in the course, or even at the start of each class, teachers can also ask students to think or write about their own intentions. This practice invites students to explore the core values they care about and build a sense of purpose.

YOU JUST NEVER KNOW

It's the fourth marking period, and Amber can sense her students' declining interest in school. She's feeling a little worn out as well. Even though the level of energy has changed, there's still a lot of work to do, especially in preparation for the final exams. Amber regularly begins the class with a mindfulness practice, but now she questions whether or not she should use this time for another review period. There's so much to cover by the end of the year! Plus, her students seem uninterested, and she doesn't feel like pushing them more than she has to.

Even though she struggles with her own motivation and attention, she decides to practice with the group, reminding herself and her students that intention is also like a muscle. It needs to be strong both in easy and more difficult times. After the class is over, one student stops to share something with Amber.

I wanted to tell you that doing the mindfulness practice every day is really helping. My mom's been sick, and she just found out she needs to have surgery. She's pretty upset. Anyway, I thought mindfulness could help her, so I told her about what we do in class, and I showed her how to listen to the practice you posted on your teacher webpage. She really likes doing a body scan because she can sleep a little better.

Mindfulness, Contemplative Practice, and the Five Goals of SEL

Self-Awareness, Self-Management, and Social Awareness

How can mindfulness and contemplative practice infuse the five goals of SEL (CASEL, 2018)? The first three, self-awareness, self-management, and social awareness, are clearly cultivated through mindfulness and compassion practices, as described in previous chapters of this book. Another formal practice included in this chapter, called A Person Just Like Me (Practice #1), adds to the compassion practice repertoire. This practice taps students' inner resources for empathy, compassion, and perspective taking, helping them cultivate awareness of people they may not know, but who have the same experiences, needs, and wishes as they do.

Social awareness, however, should also manifest in compassionate, prosocial action. As Nobel Peace Prize nominee Thich Nat Hahn has said, "Compassion is a verb." Secondary teachers, aware of needs within their classroom, school, or community, can respond creatively by devising *projects in caring* that begin with mindful intention-setting. In this way, autonomy and competence can be exercised in the service of others beyond a small, familiar circle. As teachers know, these are potent ways to build classroom cohesion, because students who practice, plan, and work together in some altruistic effort reap the benefit of connectedness. From service projects like tutoring; environmental projects like shared gardens; and contributions from drama, arts, or writing, community fundraisers or other civic actions; meaningful group activities can be compelling life lessons. Projects need not be separate from academic goals because background research, evaluation, planning, writing, calculation, and communication may all be incorporated. Moreover, each student can find a niche, in his or her own area of perceived competence, to contribute to the whole. A compilation of contemplative reflections on a project, in writing or art, can be collected and published to document students' personal experience of the process as it unfolds. Since not all group projects, in school or in life, proceed without obstacles, mindful dialogues about emergent concerns can be useful to give students real-time experience in teamwork and in resolving conflicts compassionately. Mindful listening and speaking, addressed later in this chapter, can be helpful in this process.

Ethical Decision Making: Mindful Discernment

Some suggestions for incorporating mindfulness into responsible decision making, the fourth SEL goal, include stating facts nonjudgmentally and making ethical decisions based on care (Greenberg, 2014; Lawlor, 2016). Another way to do this in practice is to pay mindful attention to one's felt sense of decision-making in "hot contexts," which can enrich conceptual understanding about making good choices. As you recall, some adolescent decisions are made in the heat of the moment. While it is not always possible to reach adolescents when they are in the grip of real-life decisions, a mindful exercise in decision-making can offer them an advance investigation into the subjective experience they are likely to encounter in these situations. This mindful discernment practice capitalizes on the adolescent capacity for mentalizing. Its intention is to help adolescents observe more dimensions of their decisional processes than they might do otherwise, to reflect on them with curiosity and acceptance, and to bring this awareness to bear on their ultimate decisions.

In the practice section of this chapter, two scenarios are provided for mindful decision-making. Students are invited to imagine themselves facing the common yet challenging circumstances of cheating and bullying. Using mental imagery, they are guided through the process of mindful observation of body sensations, thoughts, and feelings. They are encouraged to observe the comfort or discomfort level of the situation, to reflect on the nature of their inclinations to act in some way, to contemplate the outcome of their potential responses, and to understand more deeply the pushes and pulls they experience in the moments of decision-making.

Relationship Awareness: Our Connection to Others

Relating to others in healthy and productive ways is a skill that never loses its value, regardless of age. Most often, relating to others relies on verbal and nonverbal behavior, the currency of relationship. Mindfulness practice can also infuse our social relationships, the fifth SEL goal, by cultivating the ability to speak and listen with presence and connectedness. Mindful listening and mindful speaking can be practiced just as we practice awareness of the breath, body, thoughts, feelings, movements, and so on. In the capstone experience of one sequenced mindfulness program (Broderick, 2013), students share one thing that was most important to them at the end of the program. The intention for the practice is to be fully present and engaged with the act of speaking and listening. So, as students begin to share their thoughts, speakers are asked to speak authentically, from the heart, without trying to prepare their message ahead of time. Listeners are invited to listen with openness and simply to notice any tendency to rush to judgment, to criticize, to be inattentive, or the like. The content of the communication is important, but so is the mindfulness of the speaking and listening process. This kind of structured practice can be an experiment in any class discussion.

Just as we learn, through mindfulness, to approach our unpleasant internal experience with acceptance, we can also learn to be more accepting and open to differences expressed in groups. Another way to infuse mindfulness into thoughtful dialogue comes from an application of Systems Centered Training (Agazarian, 1997), called *contemplative group dynamics* (Ladden, 2014), which fosters mindful, less reactive communication. In this structured process, class members are encouraged to stay connected to thoughts, feelings, and sensations experienced in the moment and to speak mindfully and authentically throughout a discussion. The process is intended to manage the tendency to avoid or react to differences of opinion (e.g., *That's a dumb idea*) by first establishing similarities (e.g., *I agree with that part*) before considering differences.

In a dialogic process called functional subgrouping, the teacher follows up on a student's comment by asking if others in the group can "join" with that speaker (i.e., sharing and building on a previous statement). The tendency toward defensiveness, interruption, and dominance is more contained when joining with another is scaffolded in this way. The teacher can employ the technique of asking the speaker to end with, "Anyone else?" as an invitation for the next person to speak. That individual begins with, "I can join you . . . ." or, "I also . . ." and adds to the discussion, having listened carefully to what was said before.

Mindful listening in this way requires deep concentration, so this is the practice. It's impossible to join with and build on what another student has said unless you have really heard that person. Ideally, the quality of attunement in the group increases over time. After a period of joining, differences can also be invited, but from a mindful, less reactive posture. The same question, "Anyone else?" invites others to offer different opinions or experiences. Joining or differing can be perceived at the level of body sensations, thoughts, or feelings, incorporating first-person experience into a conceptual discussion. Gradually, this process allows for integration of similarities and differences, modeling through group dialogue what happens internally in personal mindfulness practice.

The Person in Process

Whatever else is happening on the surface of daily life in secondary classrooms, you can be sure that the gradual coalescing of each student's identity is going on in ways that are seen and unseen. Beyond classroom discussion, testing, and homework lies another kind of transformation. Erik Erikson, the father of identity development theory, is often quoted as identifying the central adolescent question as, "Who am I?" Erikson, however, reportedly felt dismayed by the fact that people misinterpreted his question. Instead, he argued, the real adolescent question was, "What do I want to make of myself and what do I have to work with?" (Erikson, 1968, p. 314).

"Who am I" implies a fixed answer, whereas Erikson's original question connotes fluidity and mutability. The emergence of identity for adolescents involves serious inner work that continues over many years. Even though adults continue to change as they age, the extent of change is never quite the same as is it is at this early stage. Identity is not something that evolves on its own, but emerges after a long process that is shaped and sculpted by environmental opportunity. So, just like one's incremental mindset about intelligence, one's sense of self also grows and changes.

Part of what constitutes a well-rounded secondary education is the opportunity to explore beliefs, talents, preferences, and values. Teachers are sounding boards, stable adult mentors along the way, providing feedback to young people about their skills—but perhaps even more importantly—about their worth. Erikson's important question, "What can I make of myself" may be a placeholder for "How can I matter in this world?" The work involved in figuring out this answer is best accomplished in a safe and emotionally supportive environment that offers a lot of opportunity for exploration and help in reaching healthy self-definition. As we have seen, there are lots of reasons why teenagers feel insecure: losing the more stable frameworks of childhood, coming up short in social comparisons, imagining their newly adolescent bodies as deficient, feeling pressure in more competitive contexts, experiencing more emotionality, and craving peer relationships that may prove elusive. These are the unseen risk factors that impact how students function in classrooms.

As the resilience literature amply demonstrates, however, risk factors can be counterbalanced by protective factors (Jessor, 1992). Protective factors are the traits, characteristics, attitudes, and behaviors that reduce risk, even though their benefits may not be apparent in the short term. Like crucial ingredients in a complex, many layered recipe, protective factors combine with other ingredients of life to modify some problematic effects and amplify the positive ones. Protective effects can be interpersonal as well as intrapersonal. The interpersonal contexts of prosocial classrooms (Jennings & Greenberg, 2009), for example, serve to diminish risk for individual students and lift everyone up.

Just as adolescents need to feel that they matter, teachers need to feel their work matters, too. Being an adult authority figure in an adolescent's life may entail some hard times, when love and patience are put to the test. Sometimes adolescents' self-absorption seems impenetrable. In what may mirror adolescents' own sense of separateness, adults also can feel isolated. According to research, one of the most powerful predictors of teacher commitment to education is their own sense of efficacy, or their belief that they are making a difference (Darling-Hammond & Bransford, 2005).

Certainly, this includes competence in one's subject area, positive student feedback, and student performance–based results. But as you've read before, these are not the only outcomes we hold for our students. Other things also matter in addition to academic outcomes. We know that meaningfulness is associated with happiness and life satisfaction, so reframing our work in this context can be stress-reducing. Remembering your deepest hopes and letting them support your intentions can transform your work.

Ongoing practice in mindfulness is critical because, in this work with adolescents in process, we are playing a long game.

TEACHING THEM HOW

Minh's students are getting nervous about taking the SAT exam.

I never thought I'd need help with college anxiety before, but now I think I do, one says.

Minh decides to offer a mindfulness program for juniors after school one day a week. He invites students to sign up in order to learn more about mindfulness and to explore its potential helpfulness to them. Many students sign up to come to the first class. Some drop out, but a good number of them stick with it over the 6 weeks of meetings.

At the start of class on week 5, Minh asks the students if they are noticing anything different about themselves, either in school or out, that seems related to practicing mindfulness.

When my friend asked me to come with her, one student says, *I thought it would be silly, but now I see how it helps. A lot of the things that we stress out about are beyond our control. But this is something that helps put some things back into our hands somehow, so that we can make things better on our own.*

Another offers: *When I was younger, things didn't bother me as much, but now I know I'll be leaving home soon, and I have to get my act together. I can manage my time better if I focus and not get distracted about a lot of things.*

The rest of the students nod their heads in agreement as a third student replies: *All through school, people are always telling us "just don't stress out"—but nobody tells us how. This is teaching us how.*

Not every teacher is the same in terms of being charismatic, dramatic, entertaining, serious, or scholarly. No student will respond to every teacher in the same way. Despite our collective individual differences, we can all bring intention to our daily interactions. We can all ask ourselves the same question Erikson posed about adolescents, "What do I want to make of my work and what do I have to work with?" Regardless of the roles we play, the subjects we teach, and the unique styles we bring to our classrooms, we can all work with the power of our attention and our compassion to help adolescents live more wisely, more healthfully, more altruistically, and in a more balanced and purposeful relationship with their experience.

Reflecting on This Chapter

What are my deepest hopes for my students? Is my teaching in line with these hopes? How can I use my leadership in an authentic way to make my hopes more explicit in my classroom?

What are my intentions for making my teaching more mindful? How can I make my mindfulness practice a regular part of my day?

What possibilities exist for bringing mindfulness to others in my school (teachers, administrators, parents)? How can we support each other?

> **Questions available for download and printing at**
> **http://wwnorton.com/rd/broderick**

Begin to Practice

Practice #1: A Person Just Like Me

This practice was originally adapted with permission from Chade-Meng Tan (in Broderick, 2013, p. 159). This version follows the same structure but is a new adaptation.

Sit comfortably and close your eyes if you wish. Now bring to mind the image of a person in your life. It could be a friend, a relative, or even someone you don't know very well. It could be someone in this class or outside it. To the best of your ability, hold the image of this person as vividly as possibly in your mind.

Let's consider a few things:
This person has, at some time in their life, experienced joy, happiness, and peacefulness,
Just like me.

This person has, at some time, felt stress, physical pain, anger, or disappointment,
Just like me.

This person has, at some time, worried about their ability to be successful in some way,
Just like me.

This person has, at some time, tried to cope with stress in ways that hurt themselves or other people,
Just like me.

Keeping the mental image of this person in mind as clearly as possible, let's consider that:

This person wishes to be able to handle all the challenges in their life without losing their inner balance,
Just like me.

This person wishes to be free of stress and pain,
Just like me.

This person wishes to be happy, peaceful, and loved.
Just like me.

So now, let's allow some wishes to arise:

I wish for this person to have the inner and outer strength to help them through the ups and downs of their life;

I wish for this person to be able to treat themselves and others with kindness;

I wish for this person to feel safe, peaceful, and loved,

Because this person is a fellow human being,
Just like me.

Practice #2: Mindful Discernment of Decisions

Mindfulness can add a dimension of present moment awareness to decision making. Try exploring the thoughts, feelings, and physical sensations that you notice as part of this investigation to help you understand your own decision-making processes. Remember that this example is not about any actual situation or person; it's just an example to help you learn about what happens inside you when you are faced with certain decisions. Remember that mindfulness is about helping you become healthier and have wiser, more ethical relationships with others. Don't worry if you have many different thoughts and feelings. Sometimes these problems of real life are not easy. Just do your best to notice what's going on in your thoughts and what feelings and physical sensations are present. Be kind to yourself and also remember your vision for yourself as the person you want to be.

Mindful Decision Making #1

Take a moment to settle and focus on your breath for a few cycles.
You can close your eyes if that helps you to pay attention.

Remember that many decisions you will make in your life will be complicated. So, try to be compassionate to yourself if you find this exercise challenging.

Now, as you listen, imagine as best you can that this is a real situation and that you find yourself in the middle of it. Just try to notice any thoughts, feelings, and physical sensations you experience as you imagine yourself in this situation.

You are in your math class and it's the day of a very important test. You know that this test is worth a lot in terms of your grade.
You are seated in the back of the classroom, and your teacher asks everyone to clear their desks. He passes the papers to each student, and everyone begins to work.

Notice any physical sensations right now . . . any thoughts . . . any feelings.

The test is hard, and you are about halfway through the questions. You look up from the test to check the time.
As you look at the clock on the wall, something catches your eye. You notice that a classmate across the row from you has hidden the practice worksheet for the test under the desk, so the teacher can't see. You can see that your classmate is looking down at the answers. Notice what you feel now in your body.

What thoughts are you aware of?

What emotions are you noticing?

The classmate looks around and catches your eye. You look at each other for a moment before going back to work.
What feelings, thoughts, and sensations do you notice now?

What are you inclined to do in this circumstance?

What feelings, thoughts, and sensations do you notice with respect to this decision?

What would it be like if you made a different decision?

Mindful Decision Making #2

Use the same introduction, just adding a different scenario. You can also experiment with students writing about their subjective experience as you read the practice script.

You're standing near your locker at school before class starts with three of your friends. Everyone is talking and laughing. A new student in your grade comes up to your group and asks where a certain classroom is.

One of your friends gives the new student the wrong information, and points the student in the wrong direction.

As the new student turns away, your friends start to laugh and make
fun of the person's appearance.
It's easy for everyone to hear.
Notice what you feel now in your body.
What thoughts are you aware of?
What emotions are you noticing?
The new classmate looks back and catches your eye. You look at each
other for a moment.
What feelings, thoughts, and sensations do you notice now?
What are you inclined to do in this circumstance?
What would it be like if you made a different decision?

Tips to Take Away

Mindfulness practice cultivates balanced and compassionate awareness and
supports a sense of purpose and prosocial action. Mindfulness helps us
keep our teaching intentions in mind and is not just another task to complete during your day. Mindfulness adds value to all the dimensions of SEL,
and its practice can be infused into all aspects of teaching.

Gratitude for My Own Teachers

A Final Practice

A good deal of research has demonstrated that the intentional practice of gratitude improves well-being, health, empathy, positive relationships, and life satisfaction (Emmons & McCullough, 2003). Gratitude has also been related to decreased stress and improved teaching efficacy for secondary school teachers (Cook et al., 2017). As is the case with other prosocial attitudes and behaviors, gratitude can be cultivated. This practice calls on memories of teachers' own experience as students. It is intended to build up your reserve of wholesome habits of mind and heart so that you can share them with your students in your words, in your actions, and by your very presence.

Sitting quietly, taking a moment to find the breath in your body,
Just let your attention rest softly on the breath.

Following the movement of the breath wherever you notice it
  most clearly.

We'll let a memory help us with this practice of gratefulness.
Let the memory of a teacher in your life arise,
A person for whom you feel grateful.

It might be someone who taught you in school,
Someone you knew during your teacher training,
A colleague who helped you in your work,
A relative or friend whose "teaching" enriched your life.

It might even be a student whose presence in your life
Taught you something you needed to learn,
Something valuable about yourself,
Something meaningful about your work,
Something you have carried with you into this present day.

If you can't think of an actual person,
Just try to recall an author,
An historical or spiritual figure,
Some great teacher you admire,
Someone who touched you and helped you understand important
  life lessons.

Just hold the memory of this teacher in your mind's eye.

Recall the significance of what they taught you,
Recall how often you draw on their teaching to help you through your life.

Remember that the wisdom of their teaching came to you
Through their connection,
Their generosity,
And their care for you and others.

Let yourself experience gratefulness for their presence in your life,

Now becoming aware of any sensations in your body,
Possibly feeling of lightness or warmth,
Feelings of gentleness,
Allowing your gratitude to grow and expand.

Directing the felt sense of gratitude toward this special teacher.

And now becoming aware of yourself as a teacher,
A person who is also instrumental in the lives of many people.

Gathering the felt sense of gratefulness you experience in your body,
If that's possible for you right now,
And directing it to yourself,
As you inwardly repeat the phrases:

May I be a vehicle for others' learning and well being.

May I be strong and purposeful in my intention to help.

May I offer the kindness and inspiration to my students that was offered to me.

May I take my place in the cycle of learning and growth.

May I be fully present in caring for the next generation.

References

Agazarian, Y. (1997). *Systems centered therapy for groups. An overview of the theory and its practice.* New York: Guilford Press.

Ainley, M. (2012). *Students' interest and engagement in classroom activities.* Boston, MA: Springer.

Aloe, A. M., Amo, L. C., & Shanahan, M. E. (2014). Classroom management self-efficacy and burnout: A multivariate meta-analysis. *Educational Psychology Review, 26*(1), 101–126.

American Federation of Teachers (2017). 2017 Educator quality of life survey. Available online at https://www.aft.org/sites/default/files/2017_eqwl_survey_web.pdf

American Mindfulness Research Association (2018, July 3). Mindfulness journal publications by year: 1980-2017. Retrieved from https://goamra.org/resources/

American Psychological Association (2017. *Stress in America: Coping with Change.* Stress in America Survey.

American Psychological Association (2014). *Stress in America: Are Teens Adopting Adults' Stress Habits?*

Anderman, E. M., & Maehr, M. L. (1994). Motivation and schooling in the middle grades. *Review of Educational Research, 64*(2), 287–309.

Anderman, E. M., & Midgley, C. (1997). Changes in achievement goal orientations, perceived academic competence, and grades across the transition to middle-level schools. *Contemporary Educational Psychology, 22*(3), 269–298.

Andersen, S. L., & Teicher, M. H. (2008). Stress, sensitive periods and maturational events in adolescent depression. *Trends in Neurosciences, 31*(4), 183–191. Aspen Institute. Retrieved April 2018: https://www.aspeninstitute.org/publications/practice-base-learn-supporting-students-social-emotional-academic-development/

Aspinwall, L. G., & Taylor, S. E. (1993). Effects of social comparison direction, threat, and self-esteem on affect, self-evaluation, and expected success. *Journal of Personality and Social Psychology, 64*(5), 708–722.

Baer, R. A., Smith, G. T., Lykins, E., Button, D., Krietemeyer, J., Sauer, S., Walsh, E., Duggan, D., & Williams, J. M. G. (2008) Construct validity of the five facet mindfulness questionnaire in meditating and nonmeditating samples. *Assessment, 15*, 329–342.

Bailey, N. W., Chambers, R., Wootten, A., & Hassed, C. (2018). Commentary regarding Johnson et al. (2017), A randomized controlled evaluation of a secondary school mindfulness program for early adolescents: Do we have the recipe right yet? *Mindfulness,* doi: 10.1007/s12671-018-0936x

Barnett, M. A., Nichols, M. B., Sonnentag, T. L., & Wadian, T. W. (2013). Factors associated with early adolescents' anticipated emotional and behavioral responses to ambiguous teases on Facebook. *Computers in Human Behavior, 29*(6), 2225–2229.

Begley, S. (2007). *Train your mind, change your brain: How a new science reveals our extraordinary potential to transform ourselves.* New York: Ballantine Books.

Belfield, C., Bowden, B., Klapp, A., Levin, H., Shand, R., & Zander, S. (2015). *The economic value of social and emotional learning.* New York: Center for Benefit-Cost Studies in Education.

Bergmann, S., & Rudman, G. J. (1985). *Decision-making skills for middle school students.* Washington, D.C.: NEA Professional Library, National Education Association.

Bethell, C., Gombojav, N., Solloway, M., & Wissow, L. (2016). Adverse childhood experiences, resilience and mindfulness-based approaches: Common denominator issues for children with emotional, mental, or behavioral problems. *Child and Adolescent Psychiatric Clinics of North America, 25*(2), 139–156.

Bishop, S. J. (2008). Neural mechanisms underlying selective attention to threat. *Annals of the New York Academy of Sciences, 1129*, 141–152.

Black, D. S., & Slavich, G. M. (2016). Mindfulness meditation and the immune system: a systematic review of randomized controlled trials. *Annals of the New York Academy of Sciences, 1373*(1), 13–24.

Blair, C., & Diamond, A. (2008). Biological processes in prevention and intervention: The promotion of self-regulation as a means of preventing school failure. *Development and Psychopathology, 20,* 899–911.

Blakemore, S. J., & Mills, K. (2014). Is adolescence a sensitive period for sociocultural processing? *Annual Review of Psychology, 65,* 187–207.

Bluth, K., Gaylord, S. A., Campo, R. A., Mullarkey, M. C., & Hobbs, L. (2016). Making friends with yourself: A mixed methods pilot study of a mindful self-compassion program for adolescents. *Mindfulness, 7*(2), 479–492.

Breines, J. G., McInnis, C. M., Kuras, Y. I., Thoma, M. V., Gianferante, D., Hanlin, L., . . . Rohleder, N. (2015). Self-compassionate young adults show lower salivary alpha-amylase responses to repeated psychosocial stress. *Self and Identity, 14*(4), 390–402.

Broderick, P. C. (2013). *Learning to BREATHE: A mindfulness curriculum for adolescents to cultivate emotion regulation, attention, and performance.* Oakland, CA: New Harbinger.

Broderick, P. C., & Frank, J. L. (2014). Learning to BREATHE: An intervention to foster mindfulness in adolescence. *New Directions for Youth Development,* (142), 31–44. doi: 10.1002/yd.20095

Broderick, P. C., Frank, J. L., Berrena, E., Schussler, D. L., Kohler, K., Mitra, J., . . . Greenberg, M. T. (2018). Evaluating the quality of mindfulness instruction delivered in school settings: Development and validation of a teacher quality observational rating scale. *Mindfulness,* doi:10.1007/s12671-018-0944-x

Burggraf, S., & Grossenbacher, P. (2008). Contemplative modes of inquiry in liberal arts education. Available online at: www.liberalarts.edu.

Burrow, A. L., O'Dell, A. C., & Hill, P. L. (2010). Profiles of a developmental asset: Youth purpose as a context for hope and well-being. *Journal of Youth and Adolescence, 39*(11), 1265–1273.

Carsley, D., Khoury, B., & Heath, N. L. (2018). Effectiveness of mindfulness interventions for mental health in schools: A comprehensive meta-analysis. *Mindfulness,* doi: 10.1007/s12671-017-0839-2.

Carver-Thomas, D., & Darling-Hammond, L. (2017). *Teacher turnover: Why it matters and what we can do about it.* Palo Alto, CA: Learning Policy Institute.

Casey, B. J. (2015). Beyond simple models of self-control to circuit-based accounts of adolescent behavior. *Annual Review of Psychology, 66*(1), 295–319. 10.1146/annurev-psych-010814-015156

Casey, B. J., Jones, R. M., & Somerville, L. H. (2011). Braking and accelerating of the adolescent brain. *Journal of Research on Adolescence, 21*(1), 21–33.

Christenson, S., Reschly, A. L., Wylie, C. (2012). *Handbook of research on student engagement.* Boston, MA: Springer.

Cook, C. R., Miller, F. G., Fiat, A., Renshaw, T., Frye, M., Joseph, G., & Decano, P. (2017). promoting secondary teachers' well–being and intentions to implement evidence–based practices: Randomized evaluation of the achiever resilience curriculum. *Psychology in the Schools, 54*(1), 13–28.

Collaborative for Academic, Social,and Emotional Learning, 2018. Available online at: https://casel.org/core-competencies/

Conradt, E. (2017). Using principles of behavioral epigenetics to advance research on early–life stress. *Child Development Perspectives, 11*(2), 107–112.

Creswell, J. D., & Lindsay, E. K. (2014). How does mindfulness training affect health? A mindfulness stress buffering account. *Current Directions in Psychological Science, 23,* 401–407.

Crick, N. R., & Dodge, K. A. (1994). A review and reformulation of social information-processing mechanisms in children's social adjustment. *Psychological Bulletin, 115,* 74–101.

Dahl, R. E., Allen, N. B., Wilbrecht, L., & Suleiman, A. B. (2018). Importance of investing in adolescence from a developmental science perspective. *Nature, 554,* 441–450.

Damon, W., Menon, J., & Cotton Bronk, K. (2003). The development of purpose during adolescence. *Applied Developmental Science, 7*(3), 119–128.

Danese, A., & Baldwin, J. R. (2017). Hidden wounds? Inflammatory links between childhood trauma and psychopathology, *Annual Review of Psychology, 68,* 517–544.

Darling-Hammond, L., Bransford, J. (2005). *Preparing teachers for a changing world: What teachers should learn and be able to do.* San Francisco, CA: Jossey-Bass.

Deci, E. L. (1975). *Intrinsic motivation*. New York: Plenum Press.

Deci, E. L., & Ryan, R. M. (1991). A motivational approach to self: Integration in personality. In R. Dienstbier (Ed.), *Perspectives in motivation* (pp. 237–288). Lincoln, NE: University of Nebraska Press.

Desrosiers, A., Vine, V., Curtiss, J., & Klemanski, D. H. (2014). Observing nonreactively: A conditional process model linking mindfulness facets, cognitive emotion regulation strategies, and depression and anxiety symptoms. *Journal of Affective Disorders, 165,* 31–37.

de Vibe, M. D., Bjørndal, A., Tipton, E., Hammerstrøm, K. T., & Kowalski, K. (2012). Mindfulness based stress reduction (MBSR) for improving health, quality of life, and social functioning in adults. *Campbell Systematic Reviews, 8*(3).

de Vignemont, F., & Singer, T. (2006). The empathic brain: How, when and why? *Trends in Cognitive Sciences, 10*(10), 435–441.

Diamond, A. (2013). Executive functions. *Annual Review of Psychology, 64,* 135–168.

Diliberti, M., Jackson, M., and Kemp, J. (2017). *Crime, Violence, Discipline, and Safety in U.S. Public Schools: Findings From the School Survey on Crime and Safety: 2015–16* (NCES 2017-122). Washington, D.C.: U.S. Department of Education, National Center for Education Statistics. Available online at: https://nces.ed.gov /pubs2017/2017122.pdf

Doidge, N. (2007). *The Brain that changes itself.* New York: Viking Penguin.

Duckworth, A. (2016). *Grit: The power and passion of perseverance*. New York: Scribner.

Durlak, J. A., Dymnicki, A. B., Taylor, R. D., Weissberg, R. P., & Schellinger, K. B. (2011). The impact of enhancing students' social and emotional learning: A meta-analysis of school-based universal interventions. *Child Development, 82*(1), 405–432.

Dweck, C. S. (2017). The journey to children's mindsets—And beyond. *Child Development Perspectives, 11*(2), 139–144.

Eastabrook, J. M., Flynn, J. J., & Hollenstein, T. (2014). Internalizing symptoms in female adolescents: Associations with emotional awareness and emotion regulation. *Journal of Child and Family Studies, 23*(3), 487–496.

Eccles, J. S., Midgley, C., Wigfield, A., Buchanan, C. M., Reuman, D., Flanagan, C., & MacIver, D. (1993). Development during adolescence: The impact of stage-environment fit on young adolescents' experiences in schools and in families. *American Psychologist, 48*(2), 90–101.

Eccles, J. S., Wigfield, A., & Schiefele, U. (1998). Motivation to succeed. In W. Damon & N. Eisenberg (Eds.), *Handbook of child psychology: Social, emotional and personality development* (Vol. 3, pp. 1017–1096). New York: Wiley.

Elias, M. J., & Tobias, S. E. (1996). *Social problem solving: Interventions in the schools.* New York: Guilford Press.

Emmons, R. A., & McCullough, M. E. (2003). Counting blessings versus burdens: An experimental investigation of gratitude and subjective well-being in daily life. *Journal of Personality and Social Psychology, 84,* 377–389.

Ergas, O., Hadar, L. L., Albelda, N., & Levit-Binnun, N. (2018). Contemplative science as a gateway to mindfulness: Findings from an educationally-framed teacher learning program. *Mindfulness,* doi: 10.1007's12671-018-0913-4

Erikson, E. H. (1968). *Identity, youth, and crisis.* New York: W. W. Norton.

Felver, J. C., Celis-de Hoyos, C. E., Tezanos, K., & Singh, N. N. (2016). A systematic review of mindfulness-based interventions for youth in school settings. *Mindfulness, 7*(1), 34-45.

Finn, J. D. (1989). Withdrawing from school. *Review of educational research, 59,* 117–142.

Flum, H., & Kaplan, A. (2006). Exploratory orientation as an educational goal. *Educational Psychologist, 41*(2), 99–110.

Franca, K., & Lotti, T. M. (2017). Psycho-neuro-endocrine-immunology: A psycho-biological concept. *Adv Exp Med Biology, 996,*123–134.

Frank, J.L., Broderick, P.C., Oh, Y., Mitra, J., Kohler, K., Schussler, D. L., Geier, C., Roeser, R.W., Berrena, E., Mahfouz, J., Levitan, J., & Greenberg, M.T. (2018). Evaluating the effectiveness of a mindfulness-based curriculum on adolescent social-emotional and executive functioning: A randomized trial of the Learning to Breathe program. Manuscript under review.

Fredrickson, B. L. (1998). What good are positive emotions? *Review of General Psychology, 2*(3), 300–319.

Fredrickson, B. L. (2003). The value of positive emotions: The emerging science of positive psychology is coming to understand why it's good to feel good. *American Scientist, 91*(4), 330–335.

Fredrickson, B. L. (2013). Positive emotions broaden and build. *Advances in Experimental Social Psychology, 47,* 1–53.

Fredrickson, B. L., Cohn, M. A., Coffey, K. A., Pek, J., & Finkel, S. M. (2008). Open hearts build lives: Positive emotions, induced through loving-kindness meditation, build consequential personal resources. *Journal of Personality and Social Psychology, 95*, 1045–1062.

Galla, B. M. (2016). Within-person changes in mindfulness and self-compassion predict enhanced emotional well-being in healthy, but stressed adolescents. *Journal of Adolescence, 49*, 204–217.

García-Oliva, C., & Piqueras, J. A. (2016). Experiential avoidance and technological addictions in adolescents. *Journal of Behavioral Addictions, 5*(2), 293–303.

Goetz, J. L., Keltner, D., & Simon-Thomas, E. (2010). Compassion: An evolutionary analysis and empirical review. *Psychological Bulletin, 136*(3), 351–374.

Gogtay N., Giedd, J. N., Lusk, L., Hayashi, K. M., Greenstein, D., Vaituzis, A. C., et al. (2004). Dynamic mapping of human cortical development during childhood through early adulthood. *Proc. Natl. Acad. Sci. U.S.A.,*101:8174–8179.

Goldberg, S. B., Tucker, R. P., Greene, P. A., Davidson, R. J., Wampold, B. E., Kearney, D. J., & Simpson, T. L. (2018). Mindfulness-based interventions for psychiatric disorders: A systematic review and meta-analysis. *Clinical Psychology Review, 59*, 52–60.

Goleman, D. (2003). *Destructive emotions: How can we overcome them? : A scientific collaboration with the dalai lama.* New York: Bantam Books.

Greenberg, M. T. (2014, May). Cultivating compassion. Paper presented at the Dalai Lama Center for Peace and Education's Heart Mind Conference, Vancouver, British Columbia.

Hallowell, E. M., & Ratey, J. J. (2005). *Delivered from distraction: Getting the most out of life with attention deficit disorder.* New York: Ballantine Books.

Hayes, S. C. (1994). Content, context, and the types of psychological acceptance. In S. C. Hayes, N. S. Jacobson, V. M. Follette, & M. J. Dougher (Eds.), *Acceptance and change. Content and context in psychotherapy* (pp. 13–32). Reno, NV: Context Press.

Hölzel, B. K., Carmody, J., Vangel, M., Congleton, C., Yerramsetti, S. M., Gard, T., & Lazar, S. W. (2011). Mindfulness practice leads to increases in regional brain gray matter density. *Psychiatry Research: Neuroimaging, 191*(1), 36–43.

Izard, C. E. (1971). *The face of emotion.* East Norwalk, CT: Appleton-Century-Crofts.

Izard, C. E. (2011). Forms and functions of emotions: Matters of emotion–cognition interactions. *Emotion Review, 3*(4), 371–378.

Izard, C. E., & Ackerman, B. P. (2000). Motivational, organizational, and regulatory functions of discrete emotions. In M. Lewis & J. Haviland-Jones (Eds.), *Handbook of emotions* (2nd ed., pp. 253–322). New York: Guilford Press.

Jennings, P. A., & Greenberg, M. T. (2009). The prosocial classroom: Teacher social and emotional competence in relation to student and classroom outcomes. *Review of Educational Research, 79*(1), 491–525.

Jessor, R. (1992). Risk behavior in adolescence: A psychosocial framework for understanding and action. *Developmental Review, 12*(4), 374–390.

Johnson, C., Burke, C., Brinkman, S., & Wade, T. (2017). A randomized controlled evaluation of a secondary school mindfulness program for early adolescents: Do we have the recipe right yet? *Behaviour Research and Therapy, 99*, 37. doi: 10.1016/j.brat.2017.09.001.

Kabat-Zinn, J. (1990). *Full catastrophe living.* New York: Bantam/Dell.

Kabat-Zinn, J. (2015). Foreword to the Mindfulness Initiative Report. www.themindfulnessinitiative.org.uk.

Kang, M. J., Hsu, M., Krajbich, I. M., Loewenstein, G., McClure, S. M., Wang, J. T., & Camerer, C. F. (2009). The wick in the candle of learning: Epistemic curiosity activates reward circuitry and enhances memory. *Psychological Science, 20*(8), 963–973.

Kashdan, T. B., & Steger, M. F. (2007). Curiosity and pathways to well-being and meaning in life: Traits, states, and everyday behaviors. *Motivation and Emotion, 31*(3), 159–173.

Kendall , P. C., & Braswell, L. (1982). Cognitive-behavioral self-control therapy for children: A components analysis. *Journal of Consulting and Clinical Psychology, 50*, 672–689.

Kitchener, K. S. (1983). Cognition, metacognition, and epistemic cognition: A three-level model of cognitive processing. *Human Development, 4*, 222–232.

Kittel, R., Schmidt, R., & Hilbert, A. (2017). Executive functions in adolescents with binge eating disorder and obesity. *International Journal of Eating Disorders, 50*(8), 933–941.

Klimecki, O. M., Leiberg, S., Ricard, M., & Singer, T. (2014). Differential pattern of functional brain plasticity after compassion and empathy training. *Social Cognitive and Affective Neuroscience, 9*(6), 873–879.

Klimecki, O., & Singer, T. (2012). Empathic distress fatigue rather than compassion fatigue? Integrating findings from empathy research in psychology and social neuroscience. In B. K. Oakley, A. Knafo, G. Madhavan, & D. S. Wilson (Eds.), *Pathological altruism* (pp. 368–383). New York, NY: Oxford University Press.

Klingbeil, D. A., Renshaw, T. L., Willenbrink, J. B., Copek, R. A., Chan, K. T., Haddock, A., . . . Clifton, J. (2017). Mindfulness-based interventions with youth: A comprehensive meta-analysis of group-design studies. *Journal of School Psychology, 63*, 77–103.

Ladden, L. (2014). Contemplative group dynamics: Mindfulness in the group, of the group, with the group. *Systems-Centered News, 22*(1), 14–19.

Lamm, C., Decety, J., & Singer, T. (2011). Meta-analytic evidence for common and distinct neural networks associated with directly experienced pain and empathy for pain. *Neuroimage, 54*(3), 2492–2502.

Lantieri, L. (2001). *Schools with spirit: Nurturing the inner lives of children and teachers.* Boston: Beacon Press.

Lavelle, B. D., Flook, L., & Ghahremani, D. G. (2017). A call for compassion and care in education: Toward a more comprehensive prosocial framework for the field. In E. Seppala, *The Oxford handbook of compassion science.* New York: Oxford University Press.

Lawlor, M. S. (2016). Mindfulness and social emotional learning (SEL): A conceptual framework. In Schonert-Reichl, K., Roeser, R. W., *Handbook of mindfulness in education: Integrating theory and research into practice* (pp. 65–80). New York: Springer New York.

Leaviss, J., & Uttley, L. (2015). Psychotherapeutic benefits of compassion-focused therapy: An early systematic review. *Psychological Medicine, 45*(5), 927.

LeDoux, J. (2003). The emotional brain, fear, and the amygdala. *Cellular and Molecular Neurobiology, 23*(4), 727–738.

Lee, F. S., Heimer, H., Giedd, J. N., Lein, E. S., Sestan, N., Weinberger, D. R., & Casey, B. J. (2014). Adolescent mental health—opportunity and obligation. *Science, 346*(6209), 547–549. New York: Scribner.

Leno, V. C., Chandler, S., White, P., Pickles, A., Baird, G., Hobson, C., . . . Simonoff, E. (2017). Testing the specificity of executive functioning impairments in adolescents with ADHD, ODD/CD and ASD. *European Child & Adolescent Psychiatry*, 1–10.

Liston, C., McEwen, B. S., Casey, B. J., & Posner, M. I. (2009). Psychosocial stress reversibly disrupts prefrontal processing and attentional control. *Proc.Natl. Acad. Sci. U.S.A.*, 106(3), 912–917.

Lortie, D. (1975). *Schoolteacher: A sociological study.* London: University of Chicago Press.

Lutz, A., Jha, A. P., Dunne, J. D., & Saron, C. D. (2015). Investigating the phenomenological matrix of mindfulness-related practices from a neurocognitive perspective. *The American Psychologist, 70*, 632–658.

Lutz, A., Greischar, L. L., Rawlings, N. B., Ricard, M., Davidson, R. J., & Singer, B. H. (2004). Long-term meditators self-induce high-amplitude gamma synchrony during mental practice. *Proceedings of the National Academy of Sciences of the United States of America, 101*(46), 16369–16373.

Lutz, A., Slagter, H. A., Dunne, J. D., & Davidson, R. J. (2008). Attention regulation and monitoring in meditation. *Trends in Cognitive Sciences, 12*(4), 163–169.

Maslach, C., Jackson, S. E., & Leiter, M. P. (1996). *Maslach Burnout Inventory Manual* (3rd ed.). Palo Alto, CA: Consulting Psychologists Press.

Maynard, B. R., Solis, M., Miller, V., & Brendel, K. E. (2017). Mindfulness-based interventions for improving cognition, academic achievement, behavior and socio-emotional functioning of primary and secondary students. *Campbell Systematic Reviews*, 13.

McEwen, B. S. (2013). The brain on stress: Toward an integrative approach to brain, body, and behavior. *Perspectives on Psychological Science, 8*(6), 673–675.

McEwen, B. S. (2016). In pursuit of resilience: Stress, epigenetics, and brain plasticity. *Annals of the New York Academy of Sciences, 1373*(1), 56–64.

McEwen, B. S., & Gianaros, P. J. (2010). Central role of the brain in stress and adaptation: Links to socioeconomic status, health, and disease. *Annals of the New York Academy of Sciences, 1186*(1), 190–222.

Meaney, M. J. (2010). Epigenetics and the biological definition of gene x environment interactions. *Child Development, 81*, 41–79.

Moran, T. P. (2016). Anxiety and working memory capacity: A meta-analysis and narrative review. *Psychological Bulletin, 142*(8), 831–864.

Mrazek, M. D., Franklin, M. S., Phillips, D. T., Baird, B., & Schooler, J. W. (2013). Mindfulness training improves working memory capacity and GRE performance while reducing mind wandering. *Psychological Science, 24*(5), 776–781.

National Center for Education Statistics, 2011–2012. Available online at: https://nces .ed.gov/surveys/sass/tables/sass1112_2013314_t1s_007.asp

National Commission on Social, Emotional, and Academic Development (March 12, 2018). The practice base for how we learn: Supporting students' social, emotional, and academic development. Report available online at: https:// www.aspeninstitute.org/publications/practice-base-learn-supporting-students -social-emotional-academic-development/.

Neff, K. D. (2009). The role of self-compassion in development: A healthier way to relate to oneself. *Human Development, 52*(4), 211–214.

Neff, K. D. (2015). *Self-compassion: The proven power of being kind to yourself.* New York: William Morrow.

Neff, K. D., & Vonk, R. (2009). Self-compassion versus global self-esteem: Two different ways of relating to oneself. *Journal of Personality, 77*(1), 23–50.

Nesi, J., & Prinstein, M. J. (2015). Using social media for social comparison and feedback-seeking: Gender and popularity moderate associations with depressive symptoms. *Journal of Abnormal Child Psychology, 43*(8), 1427–1438.

Nilan, P., Burgess, H., Hobbs, M., Threadgold, S., & Alexander, W. (2015). Youth, social media, and cyberbullying among Australian youth: "Sick friends". *Social Media + Society, 1*(2), 205630511560484.

Noddings, N. (1984). *Caring: A feminine approach to ethics and moral education.* Berkeley, CA: University of California Press.

Noddings, N. (2015). *A richer, brighter vision for American high schools.* Cambridge: Cambridge University Press.

Nook, E. C., Sasse, S. F., Lambert, H. K., McLaughlin, K. A., & Somerville, L. H. (2018). The nonlinear development of emotion differentiation: Granular emotional experience is low in adolescence. *Psychological Science,* 95679761877335. doi:10.1177/0956797618773357

O'Keefe, P. A., & Harackiewicz, J. M. (2017). *The science of interest.* Singapore: Springer International Publishing. doi: 10.1007/978-3-319-55509-6

Oberle, E., & Schonert-Reichl, K. A. (2016). Stress contagion in the classroom? The link between classroom teacher burnout and morning cortisol in elementary school students. *Social Science & Medicine, 159*, 30–37.

Pace, T. W. W., Negi, L. T., Dodson-Lavelle, B., Ozawa-de Silva, B., Reddy, S. D., Cole, S. P., . . . Raison, C. L. (2013;). Engagement with cognitively-based compassion training is associated with reduced salivary C-reactive protein from before to after training in foster care program adolescents. *Psychoneuroendocrinology, 38*(2), 294–299.

Paus, T., Keshavan, M., & Giedd, J.N. (2008). Why do many psychiatric disorders emerge during adolescence? *Nat Rev Neuroscience, 9*, 947–57.

Pessoa, L. (2017). A network model of the emotional brain. *Trends in Cognitive Sciences*, doi: 10.1016/j.tics.2017.03.002.

Pharo, H., Sim, C., Graham, M., Gross, J., & Hayne, H. (2011). Risky business: Executive function, personality, and reckless behavior during adolescence and emerging adulthood. *Behavioral Neuroscience, 125*(6), 970–978.

Podolsky, A., Kini, T., Bishop, J., & Darling-Hammond, L. (2016). *Solving the teacher shortage: How to attract and retain excellent educators* (research brief). Palo Alto, CA: Learning Policy Institute.

Ravitch, D. (2010). *The death and life of the great American school system*. New York: Perseus Books.

Reddy, S. D., Negi, L. T., Dodson-Lavelle, B., Ozawa-de Silva, B., Pace, T. W. W., Cole, S. P., . . . Craighead, L. W. (2013). Cognitive-based compassion training: A promising prevention strategy for at-risk adolescents. *Journal of Child and Family Studies, 22*(2), 219–230.

Roeser, R. W., & Eccles, J. S. (2015). Mindfulness and compassion in human development: Introduction to the special section. *Developmental Psychology, 51*(1), 1–6.

Roeser, R. W., & Pinela, C. (2014). Mindfulness and compassion training in adolescence: A developmental contemplative science perspective. *New Directions for Youth Development, 2014*(142), 9–30.

Rood, L., Roelofs, J., Bögels, S. M., Nolen-Hoeksema, S., & Schouten, E. (2009). The influence of emotion-focused rumination and distraction on depressive symptoms in non-clinical youth: A meta-analytic review. *Clinical Psychology Review, 29*(7), 607–616.

Sapolsky, R. (2004). *Why zebras don't get ulcers* (3rd ed.). New York: Holt Paperbacks.

Sawchuk, S. (2014). Vision, reality collide in common tests. *Education Week*, April 23, 2014, S8–S12.

Schäfer, J. O., Naumann, E., Holmes, E. A., Tuschen-Caffier, B., & Samson, A. C. (2107). Emotional awareness in depressive and anxiety symptoms in youth: A meta-analytic review, *Journal of Youth and Adolescence, 46*, 687–700.

Siegel, A. W., & Scovill, L. C. (2000). Problem behavior: The double symptom of adolescence. *Development and Psychopathology, 12*(4), 763–793.

Silvia, P. J. (2008). Interest: The curious emotion. *Current Directions in Psychological Science, 17*(1), 57–60.

Simons, J. S., & Gaher, R. M. (2005). The distress tolerance scale: Development and validation of a self-report measure. *Motivation and Emotion, 29*(2), 83–102.

Smetana, J. G., Crean, H. F., & Campione-Barr, N. (2005). Adolescents'and parents changing conceptions of parental authority. *New Directions for Child and Adolescent Development, 108*, 31–46.

Smith, J. L., & Bryant, F. B. (2016). The benefits of savoring life: Savoring as a moderator of the relationship between health and life satisfaction in older adults. *The International Journal of Aging and Human Development, 84*(1), 3–23.

Spear, L. P. (2013). Adolescent neurodevelopment. *The Journal of Adolescent Health, 52*, 7–13.

Spear, L. P. (2009). Heightened stress responsivity and emotional reactivity during pubertal maturation: Implications for psychopathology. *Development and Psychopathology, 21* (1), 87–97.

Spinhoven, P., Drost, J., de Rooij, M., van Hemert, A.M., & Penninx, B. W. (2014). A longitude study of experiential avoidance in emotional disorders. *Behavior Therapy, 45*, 840–850.

Steinberg, L. (2014). *Age of opportunity: Lessons from the new science of adolescence.* New York: Houghton Mifflin.

Sterling, P., & Eyer, J. (1988). Allostasis: A new paradigm to explain arousal pathology. In S. Fisher & J. Reason (Eds.), *Handbook of Life Stress, Cognition and Health* (pp. 629–649). New York: Wiley.

Taffel, R. (2002). The second family: Dealing with peer power, pop culture, the wall of silence and other challenges of raising today's teens. New York: St. Martin's Griffin.

Tang, Y.Y., Ma, Y., Wang, J., Fan, Y., Feng, S., Lu, O., Yu, O., Sui, D., Rothbart, M.K., Fan , M. & Posner, M.I. (2007). Short term meditation training improves attention and self regulation. *Proceedings of the National Academy of Sciences, 104,* 17152-17156.

Tirri, K., & Ubani, M. (2013). Education of Finnish student teachers for purposeful teaching. *The Journal for the Education of Teaching, 39*(1), 21–29.

Tracy, J. L., & Randles, D. (2011). Four models of basic emotions: A review of Ekman and Cordaro, Izard, Levenson, and Panksepp and Watt. *Emotion Review, 3,* 397–405.

Twenge, J. M., Joiner, T. E., Rogers, M. L., & Martin, G. N. (2017). Increases in depressive symptoms, suicide-related outcomes, and suicide rates among U.S. adolescents after 2010 and links to increased new media screen time. *Clinical Psychological Science.* doi: 10.1177/2167702617723376.

Vogel, S., & Schwabe, L. (2016). Learning and memory under stress: Implications for the classroom. *Science of Learning, 1,* 16011; doi:10.1038/npjscilearn.2016.11; published online 29 June 2016.

Weng, H. Y., Fox, A. S., Shackman, A. J., Stodola, D. E., Caldwell, J. Z. K., Olson, M. C., . . . Davidson, R. J. (2013). Compassion training alters altruism and neural responses to suffering. *Psychological Science, 24*(7), 1171–1180.

Weng, H. Y., Schuyler, B., & Davidson, R. J. (2017). The impact of compassion meditation training on the brain and prosocial behavior. In E. Seppala, *The Oxford handbook of compassion science.* New York: Oxford University Press.

Wigfield, A., Eccles, J., & Rodriguez, D. (1998). The development of children's motivation in school contexts. *Review of Research in Education, 23,* 73–118.

Williams, J. M. G. (2010). Mindfulness and psychological process. *Emotion, 10* (1), 1–7.

Wolters, C. A., & Daugherty, S. G. (2007). Goal structures and teachers' sense of efficacy: Their relation and association to teaching experience and academic level. *Journal of Educational Psychology, 99*(1), 181–193.

Yeager, D. S., & Dweck, C. S. (2012). Mindsets that promote resilience: When students believe that personal characteristics can be developed. *Educational Psychologist, 47*(4), 302–314.

Yerkes, R. M., & Dodson, J. D. (1908). The relation of strength of stimulus to rapidity of habit-formation, *Journal of Comparative Neurology and Psychology*, *18*, 459–482.

Zelazo, P. D., & Lyons, K. E. (2012). The potential benefits of mindfulness training in early childhood: A developmental social cognitive neuroscience perspective. *Child Development Perspectives, 6*(2), 154–160.

Zelazo, P. D., Blair, C., Willoughby, M. T., National Center for Education Research (U.S.), & Institute of Education Sciences (U.S.). (2017). *Executive function: Implications for education*. Washington, D.C.: U.S. Department of Education, Institute of Education Sciences.

Zoogman, S., Goldberg, S. B., Hoyt, W. T., & Miller, L. (2015). Mindfulness interventions with youth: A meta-analysis. *Mindfulness, 6*, 290–302.

Zvolensky, M. J., & Hogan, J. (2013). Distress tolerance and its role in psychopathology. *Cognitive Therapy and Research, 37*(3), 419–420.

Zylowska, L., Ackerman, D. L., Yang, M. H., Futrell, J. L., Horton, N. L., Hale, T. S., Pataki, C., & Smalley, S. L. 2008; epub 2007). Mindfulness meditation training in adults and adolescents with ADHD: A feasibility study. *Journal of Attention Disorders, 6*, 737–746.

Index

Note: Italicized page locators refer to figures or illustrations.

About the Author

Patricia (Trish) Broderick, Ph.D., is a research associate at the Bennett-Pierce Prevention Research Center at Penn State University, founder and former director of the Stress Reduction Center, and professor emerita at West Chester University of Pennsylvania. She holds a Master's degree in Counseling from Villanova University and a Ph.D. in School Psychology from Temple University. She is a licensed clinical psychologist, certified school psychologist (K–12), certified school counselor (K–12), former secondary school teacher, and a graduate of the Mindfulness-Based Stress Reduction (MBSR) advanced practicum at the Center for Mindfulness at UMASS Medical Center. She was a member of the Contemplation and Education Leadership Council of the Garrison Institute and a current member of American Mindfulness Research Association (AMRA) Practice Board. Dr. Broderick has taught courses in Stress Management, Mind-Body Health, and Human Development to undergraduate and graduate students. Her research interests include mindfulness interventions for adolescents, teacher training in mindfulness, and adolescent coping styles. The fifth edition of her developmental psychology textbook, entitled *The Life Span: Human Development for Helping Professionals* (Broderick & Blewitt) will be published by Pearson Education in 2019. She is also the developer of a research-based mindfulness program for adolescents called Learning to BREATHE published by New Harbinger (www.learning2breathe.org).